BARGES & BREAD

To Tam for his encouragement, for keeping the housework under control and for sorting out the fiddly computer stuff for me.

Barges & Bread

Canals & Grain to Bread & Baking

Di Murrell

Di & Tam Murrell, on the Lime Juice run in 1971.

PROSPECT BOOKS

2017

This edition published in 2017 by Prospect Books at 26 Parke Road, London, SW13 9NG

© 2017 Di Murrell

British Library Cataloguing in Publication Data:
A catalogue entry for this book is available from the British Library.

ISBN 978-1-909248-51-9

Set in Adobe Garamond Pro and Cochin by Catheryn Kilgarriff and Brendan King.

Printed by the Gutenberg Press Ltd., Malta.

Contents

Preface

I have always been water bound. Not any old water though and never that far, physically, from home. My water has been that of the rivers and canals of the United Kingdom and mainland Europe. Living, working and travelling on and around such waterways has given me some small insight into the lives of those whose job it once was to put bread upon our tables.

Born close to the Thames at Kingston in Surrey, I grew up with the river as a constant presence in my life. I learned to swim in it, rode my bike beside it, and celebrated birthdays with pleasure boat trips upon it. Later, I lived on boats and became interested in those whose working lives revolved around the water. Later still, I started working freight-carrying craft myself and became involved in the politics of inland waterways, campaigning against the loss of river transport, and was instrumental in re-introducing, for a while, upriver grain traffic. During this time I got to know some of the remaining few whose lives had been spent afloat: bargemen, boatmen, dockers and lightermen. I heard their stories and admired their skills. It was sad to see this life and these people disappear with almost nothing to mark their passing.

I am also a cook. Not the greatest, but good enough and always interested in the food I buy, its provenance, its source and its history. When I write on the subject of food, my life on the water always seems to intrude. I have always enjoyed baking bread. The measured way that each stage of the bread making process is achieved reminds me of our time in freight carrying. I can discern the similarities in both, those flurries of activity getting the boat ready for loading, the loading itself and then the unloading, and in between, the slow but steady progress towards our destination. The idea that I might write something which straddled and encapsulated both passions was the reason this book was born.

Di Murrell
June 2017

Introduction

History is a funny thing; it goes back a long way and often seems to have little relevance to one's own busy daily round. Only when memory develops and we have a past of our own does the notion of 'history' have any meaning. With age comes an awareness that the significant events which occur in our lives – and the way in which we interpret them – are what shape and define our personalities, and how we perceive the world around us. Similarly, our external history, by which I mean that of the world we are born into and are part of, is the chance reality that conspires to shape our wider environment. It, too, is subject to interpretation. The meanings assigned to historic events vary, depending upon the mindset of the interlocutor and their particular vantage point in time. Nevertheless, 'the past' serves as the backdrop to our temporal existence; it gives us a handle on our lives in the present and propels us into the future.

This is not supposed to be a polemic about what history is or is not. Rather it is just a description of how it seems to me. The history we are often taught revolves around the power struggles of church, state and crown; we learn about the politics of the times and grand ideas. Yet it is so often reduced to no more than a litany of occurrences, events and personalities; it can be hard to see how such a list has relevance to the lives we lead today.

My proposition is simple: I want to understand my relationship to the past and its relationship to me. I know that all of my forebears must surely have been the very smallest of the cogs that drove the bigger wheels. Nevertheless, these bit players had their own traditions and knowledge, their trades and skills, their ways of being and means of survival that must have been passed on, largely unrecorded, from one generation to the next. I would like to understand their contribution to history.

Luckily for those of us with a curiosity for the more mundane aspects of the past, there are historians who are prepared to beaver away in rooms below the castles of the high-born, the edifices of the state, and the bishops' palaces. They delve into the narrow alleyways of human history that run beneath and reconstruct the daily lives of ordinary people. They connect with the periods they study and demonstrate the way, in whatever era it occurs, that change begets change. They show how, from ideas and inventions, consequences arise – both the expected and, frequently more interestingly, the unintended. They describe how philosophies are advanced, beliefs are fashioned, and ideologies take hold. Historians worth their salt make connections. They show us how we progress through time and space. The best of them connect the then with the now and vice versa. That's my kind of history, something which resonates on an individual level, revealing the bits which have significance for me. I am motivated to find the connections between the various strands within my life and the greater world without, to discover what moves me, why I am what I am, to find my own small place in the passage of time.

The idea behind this book probably began long ago in an abstract kind of way whilst I was kneading dough on a floured board at the kitchen table. I lived on a boat then and could look out onto the river as I worked. Barges, both laden and empty, passed my window on their various ways to unknown destinations. I wondered about where they might be going and the lives of those on board. Later, once baked, the fragrance of the bread was so evocative – warm, wheaten, yeasty, still wrapped in the smell of the oven – it engaged all the senses. Without my knowing it, these two elements, bread and water, life's essentials, were insidiously entwining themselves around my subconscious, lurking in the background of a demanding and time-consuming everyday existence before eventually emerging to become the defining areas of my life.

My earliest memory: a graphic image of a round white bowl with squares of soft white bread soaking up the warm white milk poured over it, slowly dissolving the sprinkling of crystalline white sugar on top. The bowl is set on a green oilcloth-covered table with a small spoon beside it. A chair faces the bowl, seat raised higher with a cushion or two. It is for me. Smokey Joe, my tortoiseshell cat weaves himself backwards then forwards around the table legs

Introduction

with tail held high. He's waiting for the tiny child to climb onto the chair, to take up the spoon, to eat, anticipating the remains that will be placed before him in good time.

The image hangs there like a dusty painting on a wall. There are others: memories of buying bloomers at the baker's, still warm, and tearing off the forbidden crusty corners to eat as I ran home; of eating soggy sandwiches on rainy school outings beside the sea; of making toast in front of the range in the tiny back cabin of a working canal boat. Later still, I would frequently bake my own bread – marvelling at the time it took to make and the speed at which it disappeared into the mouths of a growing family.

Other connections came later and more obviously. We became barge owners and operators dedicated to preserving at least some commercial activity on inland waters. For a while during the 1980s, we were responsible for the revival of barge traffic in grain between Tilbury Grain Terminal and the River Wey. We worked barges attached to a mill which was still, after hundreds of years, harnessing water from the river to grind the flour which made the bread that London ate. Thus did my own life, albeit in a tiny way, contribute to and become absorbed into a greater story.

Consider the constancy of bread, its staying power throughout millennia, how little changed the basic product really is. Few foods are totally sufficient in themselves, but grain has sustained life wherever it will grow. And although today some fuss and fidget and worry about its effect on them, I've never heard of anyone who didn't actually like bread. Reflect, too, on the recent renaissance in bread making and baking. It has come back to the home, it has returned to the hands of the artisan baker. After nearly a hundred years as a factory-made comestible parading itself as bread, its decline into travesty and tragedy has, hopefully, been arrested. Proper bread is again appreciated and valued for the wonderful life-affirming invention that it is.

This book is mainly an account of a particular grain and its journey from source to table. My focus has been on the part water plays, both in that journey and the processes which turn wheat into the bread we buy or make to eat. The total narrative is too huge and would take too long to tell, so here instead is a more local history: how grain was brought to London to feed the people there. Historically, it was mainly by means of water – the River Thames – that wheat was transported from harvested fields to the tables of London. The story of London, its growth, its stability, its importance, has always been predicated on the Thames. It has been the Thames which has traditionally kept Londoners supplied with their daily bread. Bulk commodities, of which grain is typically one, have been moved by water for centuries. The history of this movement is long and fascinating, as are the lives of those who worked the craft, and the development of the craft themselves.

I want to explore the ways in which a centralized, constantly growing population caused the trade in grain to adapt and develop, and conversely how the needs of a city determined where and how much grain was grown. Sometimes changes in supply are brought about by events which radically disrupt daily life: plague, environmental events, wars. At other times it is invention, religion, or politics which causes a population to modify and adapt to change. Yet whatever the causes of turmoil, people must still eat to survive and traditionally they have always been dependent upon a constant supply of bread.

From the transport of wheat by water we are inevitably led to its transformation by water into flour. For centuries milling depended on water to provide the energy needed to turn the great grinding stones which processed the grain. The story of water mills, particularly of tide mills, is fascinating. These mills, fed and worked by water, became an essential industry in London, providing the flour to bake the loaves upon which those who lived and worked there depended. Finally, it is in the bakery that the last chapter in the story of bread takes place, where the skills of the baker transform a basic mix of flour and water into the bread we eat.

The story of bread has been told many times but there are still, hopefully, a few new things to be said about it.

Chapter One

A Word about Bread

Wheat, barley and rye are types of grass and wherever grass will grow in the temperate climates of the world, some form of baked grain is the staple food of the people. How a grass seed came to be the basis for man's survival and his future development must begin with conjecture. When, for instance, did man first make and eat something recognisably the precursor of that which we eat today? Perhaps it would have been no more than ground up bits of grain seed mixed to a paste with water and then subjected to enough heat to dry it out. Here, in essence, is the basic recipe for making bread and it is probably the first food recipe ever to exist.

Studies of human diets today suggest that cooking is an essential process because raw food alone cannot supply sufficient calories. The inclusion of cooked cereals in the food we eat was an important step in human evolution. Assuredly there was a period of unquantifiable length during which man must have found the seeds of wild grasses, eaten them in their raw state and gradually discovered their special properties – and this long before his more sophisticated descendants worked out that to properly produce a form of sustenance, one must harvest the cereal, separate the grain from the husk, crush the grain into flour, mix it with water and then bake it.

It requires a high degree of technical complexity and culinary manipulation to turn grain into a high energy food rich in carbohydrates. Bread is not a simple product, and yet it is the most widely consumed single food of all time. Not only is it an important source of energy, it is also portable and compact, which helps to explain why it has been an integral part of our diet for thousands of years. Most recent evidence suggests humans started baking bread at least 30,000 years ago.[1]

The controlled use of fire gave early man the ability to regularly eat cooked food which was softened by the process. This not only led to improved nutrition from cooked proteins but also changed his facial structure, his jaw, his teeth and digestive system. Cooking food made it more digestible and may even have speeded up the development and expansion of his brain. Ultimately, it was the collective use of grain, water and fire which transformed man from hunter into herdsman, from forager into farmer, from an instinctive beast whose main pursuit was finding enough food to stay alive to a being with the time to think. The production of food, rather than its acquisition, was the key to the evolution of civilization and technology.

Wheat – a staple cereal – in its natural form as a whole grain, is a rich source of vitamins, minerals, carbohydrates, fats, oils and protein. Bread provides us with more energy value, more protein, more iron, more nicotinic acid and more vitamin B1 than any other basic food.

All types of bread are a fundamental source of energy because they are rich in complex carbohydrates. The human body slowly digests these carbohydrates, turning them into sugars which, combined with oxygen in the cell's mitochondria, is what the body uses for energy, its prime source of fuel.

Bread also contains fibre, a type of carbohydrate that is indigestible, though it still plays an important role in the body's processes. Breads can contain both soluble and insoluble fibres. Soluble fibres create a gel-like substance in the digestive tract which blocks the absorption of bad cholesterol into the bloodstream and helps with blood sugar regulation. Insoluble fibre improves the health of the digestive tract by providing bulk, which aids the body's digestive and waste elimination systems and thus contribute towards keeping one healthy. Fibre moves through the body slowly, causing one to feel full faster, and satisfied for longer.

Today the nutritional reasons why bread is such a life-affirming food are well understood. To early man and his descendants all he was likely to know was that it filled him up, gave him strength and kept him healthy in a way that no other single food could do.

Socially it has served as a marker of status even as far back as ancient Roman times: 'To know one's place is to know the colour of one's bread.' So wrote Juvenal, who lived sometime during the first and second centuries AD.[2] The type of bread one ate and the amount of grain it might contain was determined by one's standing: the lowly peasant's daily bread was more likely to be made from three parts ground peas or acorns to one part grain, and was uniformly dark brown. His masters aspired to the finest, whitest of wheat breads. In times less rich in material culture than our own, moving away from the breads linked with poverty towards the more refined wheat-based breads of the social elite was often the first sign of increasing personal wealth. The love of bread made from fine wheat flour seems to be a constant over time, and is universal. Even today wheat is the single biggest agricultural crop in the world and most of it is ground into pure white flour.

Housekeeping records show that in England the average lordly household, consisting of the extended family, servants and other workers, allowed everyone about two to three pounds of wheat bread a day.[3] A prosperous peasant in the fourteenth century would also probably consume two or three pounds of bread per day, though his bread would normally contain a high proportion of rye, oats or barley. In general, the medieval peasant had much greater calorific needs than modern man. Research indicates that he burned between 4,000 and 5,000 calories per day; his typical daily diet delivered between 3,500 and 4,500 calories. Work days could last as long as 12 hours in the summer, when he might eat as much as two loaves of bread every day; 2,200 to 3,000 calories of the energy he needed came from bread alone.

The price and availability of grain, particularly wheat, is a gauge of a country's prosperity and the well-being of its people. Historically a primary task of government has been to ensure a steady and reliable supply of food, and to level out fluctuating harvests. Laws are passed to control supply and demand, to maintain standards, and to stabilize prices. Uprisings by the common people have almost invariably been predicated upon the availability of bread and as such persist even into modern times. 'Bread, Freedom and Social Justice' was the chant of the people in Egypt and surrounding Arab countries in 2011 after the bread riots which had shaken these countries to their core.

Whilst all the above is surely reason enough for why bread came to be the staple food in mankind's diet, it does not explain its social and emotional significance, which goes well beyond its value as sustenance. It has always played essential roles in religious rituals and secular culture. Reference to bread is found in proverbs, colloquial expressions, prayer and in the etymology of words. The spiritual, almost magical, status of bread has remained constant. From its beginnings, bread has held a special, even sacred sway over mankind. It is the 'staff of life', though in spite of this analogous depiction of the straight stem topped by a curling ear of corn, the complete answer is not to be found in just the grain itself, but rather in the leavening process that takes place during its making and baking.

It is commonly said that the wheel was one of man's greatest inventions, yet the tricky thing about the wheel was not conceiving of a cylinder rolling along on its edge, it was working out how to connect a stable, stationary platform to that cylinder. The stroke of brilliance was not so much in the invention of the wheel but in the invention of the axle. The wonder of the wheel is based upon the axle; the wonder of bread is based upon the leavening. Though bread itself is thought of as man's great achievement in overcoming hunger, it is the leavening process which gives bread its extra value as a foodstuff and the reason why it is so resonant symbolically. The reverence attached to bread is about something well beyond a basic mix of flour and water. It is to do with the way in which, mysteriously, without the touch of man's hand, left to its own devices it increases in size and fluidity. It seems to have a life of its own. This miraculous occurrence must have seemed in earlier times even more so, because it was repeated on a daily basis. One can see every reason to give anxious thanks to God that such a miracle might continue.

Leavening is what makes bread rise to become a light and fluffy loaf. The most common leavening for bread is yeast. Yeast is all around us, floating in the air. The first leavened bread was likely the result of some passing yeast settling in a bowl of gruel. The yeast began eating the sugars present in the softened grain and excreting CO_2, producing bubbles that resulted in lighter, airier bread.[4]

The fact that bread dough, if left for a period, increases in size must have been a matter of great wonder. It is indeed a kind of magic and even the artisanal bread-maker of today is fascinated by the process. In earlier times all sorts of beliefs and assumptions must have grown up around the rising of the bread. Not only did the basic dough increase considerably in size – and in the baked result even more so – it tasted much better too. Why not regard that as a gift from the gods? Surely most of us still do?

As it happens, wheat produces the best flour for baking bread and has always been the most desirable grain for those who could afford it. Only wheat contains the gluten that is essential to a risen loaf. Without the addition of some wheat, grains such as oats, barley and rye produce a bread that is heavy and dense.

Though many today may prefer the more interesting taste of a rough, stone ground, mixed grain loaf, in the past it was the pure white flour from the centre of the wheat grain – which made the lightest, softest and airiest bread – that was held in the highest esteem and liked the best. The science that underlies this type of bread is well understood nowadays: the wheat grain contains gluten, the substance which gives the dough its elastic quality. The more bread is kneaded then left to rest, the more gluten is released and the stretchier the dough becomes. The starch in the flour freed by the kneading process turns to sugar and the yeast feeds upon it. Thousands of little gas bubbles are generated. The starch which reinforces the gluten also absorbs water during the baking. It is the action of yeast and the release of gluten which causes the bread to rise and to become light and airy. When the dough is placed in a hot oven the yeast continues to feed on the sugars and the pockets of gas expand. As the temperature in the baking loaf rises, the yeast eventually dies, the gluten hardens and the dough solidifies.

Yet this knowledge is only relatively recently acquired. Since the beginning of time, risen bread has always held a mystery, has been surrounded by a sense of mystique, some elements of which – in spite of scientific explanations – still survive to this day.

The First Breads

Flatbreads are the earliest breads made by humans. The most basic wa an unleavened mixture of flour, water and salt that was kneaded into a pliable dough, before being shaped by hand and baked.

Evidence suggests that prehistoric man had long been able to make a form of porridge: a gruel of crushed grains and water. Even before he knew how to make simple containers for cooking, this gruel-like mixture could be turned into a form of bread, edible and sustaining. Pounding and grinding the grain using indented stones whose natural shape formed a shallow bowl was the earliest form of milling. This way of using of stones might be thought of as the first kitchen implement, the precursor of the pestle and mortar – a utensil still in common use to this day. By this method, the grinding of the grain would result in a rough flour. Once water was added and the pounded grain mixed to a gluey consistency, the resulting paste could be shaped into flat discs and then baked to a solid on the hot stones surrounding the fire. It is thought that this type of flatbread was being made and eaten at least 30,000 years ago, possibly even earlier, and would have been the first bread known to man.

Throughout the ages, and even up to the present day, flatbreads have been a staple source of food, eaten at every meal, functioning as plates for other foods served on them or as implements to scoop up liquid stews or sauces. Flatbreads are still important amongst the people of India and the Middle East, and their modern interpretations in the form of pitta, tortilla and pizza have spread to many countries.

A Word about Bread

The development of leavened bread almost certainly has prehistoric origins too, although the earliest archaeological evidence of its existence is to be found in ancient Egypt. Yeast spores occur everywhere, including on the surface of cereal grains; any dough left to rest for a while will become naturally leavened. One assumes this was simply another chance discovery: a round of flatbread ready prepared for baking but then left for some time, perhaps because of some local disturbance or family emergency, is found to have risen slightly and even grown a little larger. Not wishing to waste it, the bread is placed on the hot stone to bake and the result is a lighter, tastier and more digestible bread. Though the science behind this risen bread would not have been understood, the desire to replicate such a fine morsel would surely have led to experimentation.

Some Early Recipes

The custom of eating raw grains has prevailed for thousands of years. The Bible serves as a useful source of handed-down history, recounting the lives of people and events that happened long before they could be recorded in written form. The references to bread are frequent and reflect its importance in the diet of ancient peoples; the law of Moses states: 'Ye shall eat neither bread, nor parched corn, nor green ears, until the selfsame day that ye have brought an offering unto your God.' The disciples of Jesus ate raw grain in the fields. They 'plucked the ears of corn, and did eat, rubbing them in their hands'.

Parched Grain

This is an ancient foodstuff and is thought to be one of the earliest ways in which the hunter-gatherers in the Fertile Crescent carried and ate grains. Historically, it was a common food in the Middle East and the Bible scriptures show that it has been used for centuries. It is still eaten today in a number of countries, often served before a main meal. Offering a food full of filling carbohydrate before eating protein, fish or meat is common to many people. Consider the tradition of eating Yorkshire pudding before the roast, or pasta before the meat course. All have the effect of taking the edge off hunger.

Parched bread is simple to make. Parching is done using grains of wheat that are not fully ripe. They are dry roasted in a very hot pan or on an iron plate. When the grains brown and begin to pop, they are ready.

Grain in this form keeps well and could be easily carried, serving as an instant source of food to anyone on the move. The Bible tells us that Jesse sent David with some to his sons in the army; Abigail included it in her present to David; and David received it from friends when he fled from his son, Absalom.

The Bible also states: 'On the day after the Passover, on that very day, they ate some of the produce of the land, unleavened cakes and parched grain.' And: 'Now Boaz said to her at mealtime, "Come here, and eat of the bread, and dip your piece of bread in the vinegar." So she sat beside the reapers and he passed parched grain to her; and she ate and was satisfied, and kept some back.'

FLATBREAD

It seems hardly necessary to include a recipe for the most basic of breads – a simple mix of roughly ground flour, salt and water – but this one here is so clearly a direct descendent I think it appropriate to include.

This recipe is for the traditional Norwegian unleavened bread. It is dry, flat and crispy and, nowadays, usually only baked for the Christmas season. It can be made with any combination of flours, even pea flour or potato flour. An essential part of the Norwegian diet for a thousand years, probably even longer, but certainly from the time of the Vikings, this flatbread was originally baked on hot stones.

The quantity below makes a lot of flatbread. It can be stored in a dry cool place and keeps for a very long time. Fresh flatbread is nice but it improves with age.

Ingredients:
375 g (13 oz) brown flour
250 g (9 oz) fine white flour

A Word about Bread

1 dessertspoon of salt
½ litre (1 pint) of sour milk (unpasteurized)
barley flour for kneading

Mix the dry ingredients together in a bowl. Add the milk, stir and mix really well. It will naturally be a little wet – closer to a paste than a dough. Ideally allow it to stand for an hour or two, though of course it won't rise.

Sprinkle a good amount of barley flour onto a clean table or board and gently knead the dough to form a log. Divide the dough into pieces, so that when they are rolled out thinly each one will cover the base of the pan. While you work, cover all but the one you are shaping with a damp cloth.

Meanwhile set the frying pan over a medium heat – a 26 cm heavy-bottomed frying pan or a larger paella pan if you have one – it needs to be just hot enough to bake out the moisture in the bread. The pan also needs to be dry, so do not grease it or use any oils.

Roll out the piece of dough, scattering it with more barley flour as you roll, into a very thin sheet, the thinner the better. All the water needs to evaporate from the dough while it is in the pan – if it is too thick it will burn beforehand. Unfortunately when the dough is so thin, it is hard to handle. Use the rolling pin to pick up the dough: roll the dough onto it from one end and then carefully roll it off into the heated pan.

Once in, it will take only a minute or two for the bottom to harden. Then it can be flipped over. Dust off the excess barley flour with a cooking brush. If the dough becomes golden brown on both sides but the inside is still moist it means it wasn't rolled out thinly enough. Never mind – take the flatbread out and put it on a wire rack, it can be finished off in the oven later. Any barley flour left in the pan should be brushed out before starting the next batch.

Repeat with each lump of dough – roll out, pan bake, brush away and set on a rack. It can be useful to have a two-person team working and two pans on the go. One person can do the rolling while the other does the baking.

To finish off any pieces that didn't quite dry out during the baking process, turn the oven on at its lowest setting. If the oven seems too hot leave the door open slightly. Place the flatbreads directly onto oven shelves and allow them to gently dry out. Monitor the crispness and when ready take them out to cool.

Hand rolled flatbread can be uneven; sometimes parts of the bread may be a little chewy when fresh. The best solution is leave it out to dry for a couple of days. Nibble a piece each day to check, but don't worry about staleness; flatbread needs to mature to be at its best. When it is completely dry store in a large airtight container.

Flatbread is broken up into pieces to be eaten. It can be used as a side for soups and stews, especially fish. In Norway it is eaten with charcuterie, cheeses, both hard and soft, or spread with jam, sour cream or mayonnaise. It is also good with savoury dips, or just served spread with butter. It can even be broken up into bite-size pieces and eaten as a breakfast cereal with milk and honey.

They say 'Old habits die hard' and this may well be one. Is it possible that the open sandwich, so beloved in Scandinavian countries, where everything is piled onto one layer of bread, could be the direct descendant of this ancient flatbread?

ESSENE BREAD

Essene bread is one of the earliest forms of bread; its recipe one of the earliest recorded ways of making it. The first herders of cattle, people still making the transition from the nomadic life to that of settled farming, could easily have carried grains with them or collected them en route. The bread, once made, could be baked on scorching hot rocks in the sun. It is a dense and heavy bread, sweet and filling, which can be cut into thin slices.

The Essenes, a Jewish religious group that flourished from the second century BC to the first century AD, are credited with the technique and basic recipes for Essene bread, although no scholarly evidence exists for this claim and given its extreme simplicity it is likely to be far older than the dates ascribed to it. It derives its name from a recipe of the ancient Essenes as recorded in 'The Essene Gospel of Peace', purportedly a first century Aramaic manuscript:

A Word about Bread

'How should we cook our daily bread without fire, Master?' asked some with great astonishment. Jesus replied: 'Let the angels of God prepare your bread. Moisten your wheat, that the angel of water may enter it. Then set it in the air, that the angel of air may also embrace it. And leave it from morning to evening beneath the sun, that the angel of sunshine may descend upon it. And the blessing of the three angels will soon make the germ of life to sprout in your wheat. Then crush your grain, and make thin wafers, as did your forefathers when they departed out of Egypt, the house of bondage. Put them back again beneath the sun from its appearing, and when it is risen to its highest in the heavens, turn them over on the other side that they be embraced there also by the angel of sunshine, and leave them there until the sun be set.'[5]

Nutritionally, Essene bread is a rich resource. Made from 100 percent sprouted grain, it contains much of the goodness of the sprouts themselves – low in fat, abundant in protein, natural sugars, fibre, vitamins and minerals, all made very digestible by the presence of numerous enzymes in the sprouts. Heat is an enemy of many vital elements in food. Cooking, especially at high temperatures, can destroy high proportions of vitamins and enzymes. Because Essene bread is baked at low temperatures (90-135°C / 200-275°F) the chance of nutrient loss is correspondingly less.

To make it, the only required ingredient is sprouted wheat grain, though it is important to use whole grains with the germ and bran intact. They should not be hulled, husked, pearled, rolled, flaked, or otherwise altered. Wheat grain for sprouting is easily found in wholefood shops and hard wheat grain is preferable to soft.

To Sprout the Grain

1 to 2 cups of whole wheat grains will produce 4 to 6 cups of sprouted.

Rinse the grains in cool water, drain, then place them in a large bowl and cover with cold water. Cover the bowl with a plate or cloth and allow the grain to soak at normal room temperature overnight or for about 12 hours. They will soak up a considerable amount of water. Drain them in a colander, pick through them discarding any that are unsprouted or discoloured, cover the colander with a plate to prevent the grain from drying out, and put it somewhere away from direct light. Rinse the grains about three times a day and they will soon begin to sprout. After two or three days the sprouts will reach their optimum length of about ¼ inch. Speed of growth depends on moisture and temperature; be patient.

To Make the Bread

Once the wheat has sprouted it needs to be ground. Although the resulting mush might be closer to the original were it mashed up using the time-honoured and more authentic pestle and mortar, it is easier to grind the sprouted grain in a food mill, whizz in a food processor, or use a slow juicer with a mincing cone attached. The resulting dough should be juicy, sticky, mottled light and dark and have the consistency of raw mincemeat.

After grinding, drop the grain mash onto a clean work surface. Wet your hands and squeeze and knead for no more than 10 minutes. Form small round, hearth-style loaves with your hands, two good handfuls to a loaf. Sprinkle an insulated baking sheet with a little bran or cornmeal, and put the loaves on it. If you wish, you can cook them straight away or they can be left in a warm spot, like an airing cupboard, for 12 to 24 hours, covered by a light cloth. Left to itself, it can double in size, sometimes more if the grain has been finely minced.

Raw Version

Essene bread baked in the traditional way, on hot rocks in the scorching sun, may not be a feasible option for many of us today, though if you find yourself in the middle of a serious heat wave you might give it a try.

In this version, the bread is slow-cooked for a total of 24 to 36 hours. It can be left out in hot sun or baked in a very low oven at a maximum temperature 40°C / 104°F for much the same length of time. At this temperature the high level of enzymes and other nutrients will be retained, producing a very digestible and healthy loaf.

Cooked Version

Alternatively the loaves can be baked in an oven. Bake for approximately 2 ½ hours at 130°C / 250°F / Gas ½ – until the outside feels firm (but not hard) and the bottom when pressed with a thumb feels springy. The inside will be soft, developing a firmer texture as it cools. To prevent them drying out while baking, a pan of water can be placed in the bottom of the oven.

Cool the loaves on wire racks and store in sealed plastic bags. Don't refrigerate if you intend to eat them within the next three or four days. They will stay moist if kept at room temperature. Refrigerated, the bread will keep for around four weeks and can also be frozen.

This sprouted bread recipe takes days to make from start to finish. However the time and effort is worth it with the reward of a most singular bread – solid, sweet, and moist. You can eat Essene bread with most things – it works well as an open sandwich and for a 'stone age' treat and possible authenticity I love it spread with a lick of honey.

EZEKIEL BREAD

This may well be the first survival bread recipe ever to be documented; it is one that satisfies all the body's nutritional requirements and, it would appear, is backed up by the word of God!

The recipe is in the Book of Ezekiel (4:9) so if you have a Bible you already have the recipe: 'But as for you, take wheat, barley, beans, lentils, millet and spelt, put them in one vessel and make them into bread for yourself; you shall eat it according to the number of the days that you lie on your side, three hundred and ninety days.'

God gave it to Ezekiel the prophet to help the Israelites survive famine during their three hundred and ninety days in exile. When the ingredients are combined, it becomes a complete protein meal and one which can be survived on indefinitely.

Ingredients:
2½ cups wheat whole grains
1½ cups spelt flour
½ cup barley
½ cup millet
¼ cup dry green lentils
2 tablespoons dry great Northern beans (or dry cannellini beans)
2 tablespoons dry kidney beans
2 tablespoons dried pinto beans
4 cups warm water (45°C / 110°F)
1 cup honey
½ cup olive oil
2 (¼ ounce) packages active dry yeast
2 tablespoons salt

Measure the water, honey, olive oil and yeast into a large bowl. Leave it to sit for 10 minutes. Stir the dry grains and beans together until well mixed. Grind in a flour mill or whizz in a food processor until finely ground. Add the fresh milled grain and bean flour plus the salt to the yeast mixture; stir for about 10 minutes until well mixed. The dough will look a bit like thick batter. Divide it between two greased 9 x 5 inch loaf tins and leave to rise in a warm place for about an hour, or until the dough has reached the top of the tin. Bake in a preheated oven at 175°C / 350°F / Gas 4 for 45 to 50 minutes, or until the loaves are golden brown.

Use this like normal bread or, out of interest, why not try living on it on its own for a while, though maybe not for the full three hundred and ninety days!

Chapter Two

A Population of Farmers

Daily life in the homes of settled farming communities continued by and large in much the same way for hundreds of years, before, during and long after the Roman occupation. Subsequent waves of incomers, some coming to settle peacefully amongst the existing native population and others more intent on invasion and the destruction of the prevailing order, brought many religious and political changes, but the domestic life of the mainly agrarian population of Britain seems to have been rarely disturbed. Though the ownership of land gradually shifted with successive changes in those who ruled the country, and the peasant farmer slowly lost his rights to the land he worked, eventually becoming a servant working for his lord, for many centuries his way of life changed very little, especially in the food he ate and the way he cooked it.

His basic sustenance was probably a form of gruel: a soup of vegetables and greens thickened with some form of grain. During the growing seasons, he would have access to all forms of wild plants, seeds, fruits and roots. In times of plenty, the pot of soup thickened with barley would have been tasty and nutritious. Wild meat and fish were much more accessible than they are today and though there were often strict rules governing what the peasant might take from his lord's land it is likely he would have been skilled in tracking, trapping and catching his food. He would keep an animal for slaughter even if it were only one pig. He might have a cow to milk and chickens to supply him with eggs. He would grow barley for his ale and pottage, and wheat or rye for his bread. He would dry roots and fruits and legumes, harvest the grains he had sown and store his gathered nuts to see him through the winter months. When times were hard, the result perhaps of natural disasters or climate change or catastrophe at the hand of his political masters, he might just survive on little more than a simple porridge of the crushed seeds mixed with water – provided some form of grain had been harvested and stored. The daily life of the peasant farmer and that of his family followed an invariable routine. His cultivation of grain became increasingly part of an established pattern.

The period between c.500 and 1300 saw a major change in diet. More intense arable farming on an ever-increasing acreage resulted in a shift from meat and dairy products to various grains and vegetables as the staple diet for the majority of the population. Before the fourteenth century, bread as we know it was not an everyday feature among the peasant classes, especially in the north where wheat was more difficult to grow. A bread-based diet became gradually more common during the fifteenth century and began to replace the standard porridge-based or gruel-based foods. Leavened bread was more widespread in wheat-growing regions in the south, while unleavened flatbreads of barley, rye or oats prevailed in the northern and highland regions.[1]

During the Middle Ages wheat, barley, rye and oats were the crops sown in the southern part of Britain. Of these, wheat was the most valued because it had the gluten content necessary to make good bread, though it was the one grain our peasant would rarely, if ever, taste, the bulk of it being reserved for the tables of his masters. As one descended the social ladder, bread became coarser, darker, and its bran content increased.

Barley was mainly used in the brewing of ale, though with a small addition of wheat it made a tasty loaf – and for a darker heavier bread, rye too could be added. Oats were grown predominantly for animal feed, though a basic porridge of oats would have been an almost permanent fixture in the peasant diet. All four grains were sown in autumn for harvesting the following summer. This winter crop could easily be lost to a particularly cold winter or stormy spring, so farmers would, if possible, plant a second crop in the spring. The grain was sown as soon as the land could be ploughed, generally in March, and gathered in during late summer, though with so little time to grow it rarely yielded as much as a successfully harvested winter crop.

The medieval farmer generally worked on a three-field rotation system: one field for grain, one field for hay, and a third left fallow, sown with a legume which would be ploughed under to enrich the soil. The fields themselves were long narrow strips of land which were not contiguous; all must share the same quality of land, good or bad. The soil would be enriched throughout the winter with lime, chalk, manure, and by ploughing under burnt weeds. The fields were worked with an ox-drawn plough, the seed sown by hand, and finally a harrow, a square wooden frame with wooden spikes pointing into the earth, was dragged across the field to cover the seed. Sometimes if the earth was particularly heavy it would also be used to break up the soil before the seed was sown. The crop must then be weeded once or twice in spring and summer.[2]

Harvesting began in late July for the winter crop and in late August for the spring. Ripened grain is delicate and falls easily off the stalk; it would be cut carefully with a hand sickle, bound into sheaves, and the sheaves arranged into stacks. The stacks were then brought indoors for winter storage. The grain was frequently stored, as Rachel Hartman puts it, 'just as it was, still on the stalk'. This was partly so it would draw up the last moisture from the stalk and become heavier, but also because threshing and winnowing were good indoor activities for bad weather and kept people warm and occupied throughout the winter.[3]

Hartman goes on to describe the way the grain was processed:

Threshing took place in an open area of the barn where a special wooden floor was set up. Flails were used to beat the stalks, thereby causing them to shed their grain. The straw was removed and the grain scooped up into a wide, shallow, winnowing basket. By tossing the grain into the air and fanning it, the lighter inedible chaff (inedible husks) blew away until only the heavier grain remained. The heaviest grain fell closest to the winnower and was saved to plant next season. Grain that was to be eaten was dried in a kiln and taken in sacks to the mill.[4]

In southeast England, wheat and barley became the two standard crops: wheat for bread and barley for beer, and until the arrival of local corn grinding mills, the primary household tool was the rotary quern-stone. This was used dry for grinding grain into flour, while water was added to the more coarsely ground barley to make a mash for ale.

The Earliest Milling Method

Quern-stones, like the pestle and mortar, are among the earliest cooking utensils known to man. The stones were used in pairs for hand grinding a wide variety of materials. The upper stone, called the handstone, was as the name suggests turned by hand. The lower stationary stone is the quern. The rotary quern used circular motions to grind the material, meaning both the quern and the handstone were circular – looking rather like miniature mill-wheels. The handstone of a rotary quern is heavy and provides the necessary weight for the grinding of unmalted grain into flour. In some cases the grinding surfaces of the stones fit into each other, the upper stone being slightly concave and the lower one convex.[5] The upper stone could be raised slightly to adjust the grind height to a 2-3 mm clearance, which allowed the husks from the grain to be removed.[6]

Using a quern-stone was laborious and time-consuming. It is estimated that a skilled quern-stone operator might produce three kilos of flour an hour. An Anglo-Saxon settlement of 100 people would need at least three people working 10-hour days to produce enough flour to supply their daily bread. It seems unlikely that this would have happened on a daily basis; more probably querns were used to produce a rough ground grain which could be boiled and eaten like porridge. People in small groups may have baked bread when they could, but relied for their daily diet on boiled crushed grain.

A Population of Farmers

Manufactured quern-stones were first used in the Neolithic period to grind cereals into flour and, like the pestle and mortar, are still to be found in use in some societies, unchanged to the present day.

The Earliest Grain Stores

Archaeologists tell us that from the earliest of times, individual households kept grain to feed themselves in pits located close to the central hearth. The grain was stored, unhusked, in bell-shaped storage pits with a small round hole on the top which would probably have been plugged with a portion of clay, followed by a covering of turf to prevent the clay plug drying out and shrinking. Grain in contact with the edge of the pit would begin to germinate and as it did so would use up any remaining oxygen and release carbon dioxide in the process. It thus created a vacuum that could keep the grain for years without deterioration.[7] Any sprouting grain can be eaten early in germination, crushed and mixed with water, or baked and turned into malt to make a light beer. The simplest daily bread could be made by throwing handfuls of the stored unhusked grain into a pot and heating it over a fire long enough to burn off the husks whilst leaving the corn uncharred.[8] It could have been winnowed, ground, and baked on the hearth stones within the hour.

It seems likely that while individual pits and later storage jars were retained for family use, they were probably only sufficient to house the annual harvest. With the development of the feudal system, any surplus grain grown by the tenant farmer went to the granaries of his landlords – the Church and the gentry.

Bread Ovens

The history of the development of ovens used to bake bread is obscure. At their simplest, Neolithic earth ovens or pits were no more than holes dug into the ground. A fire is lit in the bottom of the pit and allowed to burn until only hot coals are left behind. The walls themselves and stones placed in the fire absorb and radiate the heat back towards the centre of the pit. This heat is then used to bake, smoke or steam food inside the pit. It has been mooted that the idea for the earliest ovens may have come about as a result of an accidental discovery. After a pit oven has been constructed, the sides need to be smoothed so that it doesn't crumble when it is used. Wet hands aid the smoothing of the walls. An oven dug by chance in a clay soil, smoothed by wet hands will resemble the unbaked walls of pots. The effect of the heat in the enclosed space would be to fire the clay sides. Though not at that point freestanding, it could not have been a big step from there to making clay ovens which could be transported from place to place. Shaped patties of grain and water could be thrown against the hot sides where they would stick to cook quickly and evenly. Such ovens have certainly been in existence since prehistoric times. A direct descendant, still used today, is the central Asian tandoor.

The forerunner to our own in situ wood-fired bread oven is more obscure, though if one assumes a steady process of development over time, it is easy to see how the original clay-lined earth ovens might have been the predecessor to the wood-fired pizza ovens we know today. Like the pestle and mortar and rotary hand mills, once invented, the front-loading bread oven as employed by the ancient Egyptians, Greeks, Romans and Jews is another piece of equipment that has remained in use essentially unchanged over millennia.

Less obvious is how the oven came to be used for the baking of leavened bread, though the Egyptians are usually credited with this invention. Who knows? What is clear is that once the baking of flatbreads in ovens became an established practice, the accident of baking some bread infected with wild yeasts would have been inevitable. The first risen loaf to be removed from the oven's depths must have been like some small miracle and was indisputably the progenitor of the bread we know today.

In England, there is little early evidence of bread ovens in peasant homes. Initially houses, though heated by fire, lacked a chimney. Before the chimney, smoke from the fire, which was set on a clay or brick surface in the centre of the house, would fill the room, escaping either through a hole made for that purpose in the roof or in the wall. Cooking was mostly done in clay and iron pots hung over the open fire. Some types of bread could have been baked on iron griddles. A heavy lidded pot, nestling amongst hot embers could have been used as a baking oven. It remained the case that most enclosed houses, other than those of the landed gentry, were smoke-filled chimneyless buildings until as late as the sixteenth and seventeenth centuries.

Bread continued to be baked on hot stones and later on flat iron griddle pans over open fires – a practice that continues in some country houses to the present day. In the houses of the very wealthy, bread ovens would have been more common, and as villages became established and the urban population grew, it was more usual for the milling of flour to take place at some central point near where a bakehouse could be established, with the local population obliged to purchase their bread there. In places like London, professional bakers became the norm and records show that from the medieval period onwards this was the established practice in all urban areas. Later, as the populations of large towns and cities continued to grow, granaries and mills moved away from the towns to be built closer to the grain distribution centres that had become established further afield. The milled flour was then brought to the cities by road and water, and the bread baked in regulated bakeries and sold through local bread shops.

Recreating an Early Bread

Early bread recipes are hard to come by, and in any case original recipes tend to be obscure when it comes to describing amounts, cooking temperatures and timings. Early professional bakers rarely seem to have felt the need to record how they made their bread, presumably because it was unnecessary, their apprentices being taught on the job.

The processing of flours, especially wheat, has become much more refined in recent years. On the other hand, it is easier today to buy any number of ancient grains ground using methods unaltered since the Romans introduced the first water mills into Britain some two thousand years ago.

Some ways of cooking have also continued essentially unaltered since the earliest times. This is particularly so in the case of the breads baked in the home on griddles over an open fire, and the wood-fired bread ovens which baked the bread of larger communities. Between these two come the covered clay and iron pots used both in the home and by those on the move. Today's so-called Dutch oven is a direct descendant.

I recently came across what must be the apotheosis of all re-creations of early bread. Ken Albala is a man who surely knows his stuff, Professor of History, Director of Food Studies at the University of the Pacific (US) and a prolific writer on food history. Here is Ken's entertaining account of how he made his bread, literally from scratch:

1. Grow Your Own Wheat.

I started by growing a European low-protein wheat with a long historical pedigree. I gathered the seed by hand on a farm in Finland. I then planted the wheat in my backyard in wooden barrels. Predictably there was some rye among it, and what appeared to be a few stalks of oats. No matter, that was probably fairly typical in the past.

The wheat grew extremely well in the winter in California and I harvested at best twice the amount of wheat I had planted. Apparently I am not a great farmer, but I was nonetheless able to cut the wheat, thresh, and winnow it in a large basket by hand, more or less as would have been done in the Middle Ages.

2. Grind it by Hand.

Next came the stone grinding, which was done with a small hand quern. It took about half an hour of milling. A medieval miller would have been much more experienced than I am in 'keeping his nose to the grindstone' to prevent heating the grain too much and in separating the hull, but I was able with a few grindings and siftings to get a reasonably fine whole grained flour, a little over a pound or 5 cups.

To this was added about a cup of natural starter made only with flour and spring water, fed every day with more flour and spring water for about two weeks until the yeast and bacteria were nicely balanced and it smelled pungent. I had been using it for a month or so to make sure it was strong enough before using on the backyard flour. The starter, flour, more water and a little salt were kneaded into two loaves and each left to rise for about 3 hours, then kneaded again and placed into wicker basket forms, covered with a cloth and left to rise about 18 hours until nearly tripled in size.

3. Cook it in Your Hand-Built Oven.

Now turn back the clock about a month, when I built the wood-firing oven. I did not follow plans and was determined not to spend a lot of money either. Essentially I laid out cinder blocks on top of which I patted a slab of clay about a foot thick. On top of that I laid a refractory clay shelf, which can withstand direct flame. Then a hemispherical dome of wet sand. On top of that I laid another foot of clay all around. After letting it harden for a few days I scooped out the sand.

In retrospect, I should have let it dry completely and fired it in situ, but I decided to cut the entire thing into bricks, all carefully labeled and then fired them in a kiln. Little did I realize how hard the reassembly would be when the bricks were labeled with uppercase, lowercase, and Greek letters!

I was able to get everything back together with mortar and then cover everything with a foot's thickness of stucco. Fiberglass insulation would have made it much more efficient at heat retention, as would straw in the bricks, which would have been more historically accurate as well. In any case, the oven worked fine, easily reaching about 500 degrees, which is excellent for baking. Smaller sticks work better than heavy logs for some reason.

With about an hour or two of burn, the oven was extremely hot inside and could still be touched on the outside, meaning that it did hold the heat fairly well. Once it got hot enough I dragged the ashes out with a shovel and cleaned the floor of the oven with a wet mop.

The loaves were turned out onto the peel [a flat shovel-like implement used by bakers to get bread into and out of an oven], quickly slashed with a very sharp knife in a star pattern allowing the dough to rise upward, and finally slid into the oven. The door was closed and the loaves baked until they sounded hollow when rapped. Whether the result bears any resemblance to a medieval loaf is beside the point; I was able to experience more or less what the medieval baker would have done every day, on a larger scale. And incidentally, the bread was fabulous.[9]

Chapter Three

London and the Thames

When the Romans arrived in the Thames Valley they found a populated district of well-cultivated land, with established trading links on the Thames, both to seaward and beyond and inland to the west. Its many streams and tributaries provided water for domestic and farming purposes as well as a source of food and a means of travel and communication. Justification for conquest and occupation required rapid returns. This area of England, with its rolling arable land, was ideally suited to the growing of wheat, oats, barley and rye, which were valued items for export to other Roman provinces in the northwestern part of Europe.

The Making of London

There is evidence that there had long been a settlement perched on the hillock on the narrowest reach of the tidal river and it was blessed with two natural ports: the mouths of the Walbrook and the Fleet rivers. Here was a site practically impregnable from the land.[1] The shore from Battersea to Greenwich was then an unbroken expanse of mud, some 9 miles long and up to 3 miles wide, which was submerged by the incoming tide twice every 24 hours.

The small earlier settlement which became Roman Londinium was perfectly sited on the north bank of the Thames, at the point where the tidal flow met the inland stream. Though London was a good way from the mouth of the river, the tides provided sufficient volume and surge for ships to navigate between the port and the sea, and the constant supply of freshwater flowing downstream ensured enough depth for ships to lie at anchor in the river even at low tide. London's distance from the sea afforded it considerable protection from surprise attack even though it was situated on a river which easily connected the city with the rest of Europe and beyond. Its position on the Thames was crucial to its success.[2]

Today, where the river passes through the embankments of central London, it is forced into a relatively narrow stream. But in earlier times it was much broader and shallower here and flanked by impassable marshes, which prevented access except at one or two points; it flowed much more slowly, with a tidal range of about one metre. As modern redevelopment of London's waterfront has progressed, it has been discovered that the riverbank of the first century did not lie directly beneath the modern quayside, but was more than 100 metres inland, just to the north of Thames Street. Near the site of the present London Bridge a seam of gravel crossed the river, thus forming the first ford to be reached on the journey upstream from the estuary. Here, the river could be easily waded across at low water.

There is little doubt that the presence of this ford was a determining factor in fixing the position of the earliest settlement. The first bridge was constructed from where a sandbar on the south bank (now Southwark) faced two hills of gravel on the north bank (now Fish Hill Street). These two hills – known today as Cornhill and Ludgate Hill – provided an excellent habitable area protected on the western side by two streams, the Fleet and the Walbrook, and by forests and marshes to the north and east. The shores of the settlement were washed by 'the pool' – originally the stretch of river alongside Billingsgate on the southern side of the city but later used more generally to refer to the stretch of river from Rotherhithe to London Bridge – the furthest point navigable by a tall-masted vessel. The pool was to become London's first port; its location was of vital importance for centuries to come and was effectively the reason for London's evolution.

Here, then, was a walled city built on twin gravel hills divided by a stream whose many tributaries supplied it with clean water. It was a perfect site for a fortress town. It had dry ground for building and good visibility over the surrounding countryside. Bridging the river was an essential part of Roman Britain's transport network, both for commercial enterprise and military activity. The first London Bridge, constructed in timber as early as 50 AD, was the only bridge crossing the Thames downstream of Kingston-upon-Thames and led to the single road which ran through the marshy ground to Southwark – Watling Street. It was built at the point where the river was narrow enough to bridge, but still deep enough to allow the relatively small seagoing vessels of the time access to the pool.

By positioning the embryonic city at the river's lowest bridging point, the Romans were able to control land, sea and river communications in southern Britain. The bridge itself was maintained and guarded by a small garrison. On the high ground at the northern end, a small opportunistic trading and shipping settlement took root and quickly established itself as the town of London. Another, smaller settlement developed at the southern end of the bridge at Southwark. Though various upstream fords and ferries remained in use, it was the bridge that offered the first uninterrupted traffic of foot, horse and wheeled vehicles across the river, and it ultimately linked the four Roman-built arterial road systems north of the river to the four on the south side.[3] The river, bridge and road network formed the framework upon which the wealth of London was built.

During the Roman period, the city had a population of approximately 45,000 to 60,000 inhabitants. By the end of the first century it had become the largest settlement in Britain and soon after replaced Colchester as the capital of Roman Britain. It grew in importance during much of the Roman occupation, both as a trading and distributing centre. The evidence for this is in the development of the main roads into the interior of Britain, which to this day make London the centre of the transport system of England. It is recorded that by the end of the second century London was 'a great and wealthy city' and in the year 359 AD, eight hundred cargoes of grain were exported to storehouses on the Rhine.[4]

Here may be noted another factor of the greatest significance in the situation of London as a port: the estuary of the Thames is directly opposite the mouths of the three great Continental rivers – the Elbe, Scheldt and Rhine, natural channels of trade to the vast hinterland of Europe. Evidence suggests that during the latter two centuries of Roman rule there were basically four waterborne trade routes centred on London: the North sea and channel route bringing goods from the Rhineland provinces of Rome; the Atlantic route from western Gaul; the route down the Thames from Oxfordshire; and the coastal routes around eastern and southern Britain between the Humber and Dorset to the Thames estuary.

Simply put, without the Thames there would not have been, indeed could not have been, the city of London. Blessed with a constant supply of clean water, teeming with fish, and nestling at the centre of the most productive grain growing area in the country, it was destined, eventually, to become one of the great commercial centres of the world. Though true, such grandiose phrasing gives only a general indication as to why London was destined to become a great city and neglects to explain quite how this status was achieved. The development of London from small riverside settlement to capital city was accomplished through the creative energy of the Romans and the toil of the native population.

At its most basic level, it is people who create and manufacture the goods that others want, who build the required infrastructure and provide the necessary services. The people of London prospered, as did their enterprises, yet there was a price to be paid. These were the people who were amongst the first to lose their direct and fundamental connection to the land, the birthright of everyone in Britain before the coming of the Romans. They were no longer farmers in control of their own food supply but instead became city dwellers dependent upon others to keep them fed, to supply their daily bread. London's first citizens looked to the Thames for their very survival: it was the river that provided water for drinking and the removal of waste; the river was the means by which staple foods, principally in the form of wheat and barley, could be shipped in quantity; it was the river that could be harnessed to grind the grain which nourished the people; and it was river water mixed with flour that provided their daily bread. Ultimately it was the harnessing of the river that freed these first urbanites from the monotony and drudgery of farming life. It also provided the means to build a city.

The Making of the Port

Under the Romans, London became a major civil port trading widely with the Mediterranean countries, Gaul and the Rhine. It was a port long before it became a great city. London the capital is founded upon London the port. With the forming of this symbiotic relationship, London was able to take on a life of its own, separate in many ways from life in the rest of the country. There was, however, one essential prerequisite upon which both town and port depended – that of feeding its people. This requirement was met largely by the bountiful nature of the surrounding countryside and its hard-working farmers.

The extent of seaborne trade to London prior to the Roman occupation is impossible to gauge, but by 30 AD British exports to the Continent included skins, slaves, hunting dogs, wheat, cattle, metals, iron, silver and gold which were exchanged for ivory, amber, jewellery, glassware, pottery and household articles. High among the officials of Roman London would have been those charged with conservancy and other port duties. The Portoria, or Customs duties levied upon imports and exports, required a bureau of officials. The Roman historian Tacitus states that by 61 AD London 'was much frequented by a number of merchants and trading vessels'.[5]

After Boudicca's rebellion in 61 AD, which resulted in the emerging settlement being burned to the ground, the bulk of the port was rebuilt and the waterfront extended. It was built in four sections where ships could be loaded and imported goods landed: Billingsgate, Queenhithe, Dowgate at the mouth of the Walbrook, and Bridewell at the entrance to the Fleet.

Although quays of timber or stone probably existed in the harbour formed by the junction with the Thames and the Fleet and

Walbrook rivers, in the main ships were anchored out in the stream and their cargoes transferred to and from the shore in small boats. With the development of sturdy flat-bottomed swim-ended barges, such craft could be beached along the strands and goods loaded and unloaded directly by carts driven down onto the foreshore. This movement of goods from ship to shore, known as lighterage, was a major influence in the development of the port and its effects have lasted down to the present day.

Shipping on the River

We know little about Roman transport ships, especially those used in north European waters, though shipbuilders in the region would have built in the Romano-Celtic tradition rather than in a Mediterranean style. These northern ships were strongly built of stout oak planking, secured to timber frames with iron nails, and built with a single mast, possibly rigged with a square sail. One imagines that such vessels would have been slow and cumbersome and could not have sailed without a favourable wind. Their robust construction however was not simply to withstand sea conditions; they would need to cope with being beached on the foreshore or to take the ground while loaded.

Evidence from two wrecks found in very different places – one in Guernsey in the Channel Islands and the other in the Thames – gives us some idea of how the construction of ships had developed from earlier forms and tells us something about how ships were being used in and around Britain in Roman times. Both vessels appeared to match a native Celtic Briton type of shipbuilding rather than the traditional Roman style. The 'Blackfriars ship 1', found sunk off Blackfriars in 1962, dates from about 150 AD. This suggests an already well-established indigenous shipbuilding industry building craft in a particular fashion, though one now beginning to benefit from Roman input and innovation.

When the 'Blackfriars ship 1' collided with another boat in the Thames and sank, she was loaded with some 26 tons of Kentish ragstone, a type of very hard stone much used by the Romans in the building of London. It had loaded the stone, which came from a nearby quarry, at Maidstone in Kent, and then made its way to London via the rivers Medway and Thames. Although employed here on what must have been a regular and local traffic between Kent and London, other evidence found in the sunken vessel showed that it was also a seagoing ship. Though still without the sophistication of later craft employed in much the same way, with its flat bottom and shallow draught, the 'Blackfriars ship 1' could be considered an early forerunner of the Thames barges that continued in this type of trade right into the twentieth century.[6]

London's Granaries and Water Mills

The Romans introduced granaries with floors raised off the ground which allowed air to circulate and reduced damp. Here the wheat was stored in bulk, along with drying furnaces which prolonged its life once stored. Roman wheat was often conserved as the complete head rather than individual grains. These would be processed on a daily basis, the chaff being separated out from the wheat which could then be ground into flour as required. The granaries in London were built close to mills and to the source of their supply. This generally meant they would be found by the riverside. Grain could be brought in by barge and most likely was transported in sacks rather than in bulk form.

How the grain in a Roman granary was stored is not exactly known, but it appears likely that if it was carried in sacks on the barge, it would be stored in the granary in the same manner. Though hauling sacks of wheat out of the bottom of a barge and then carrying it into the storage area would have been labour-intensive work, throughout recorded history labour has always been the cheapest commodity, especially when in times like these it might well have been that of slaves.

Mills, both animal-powered and water-driven, had become an important part of the Roman economy. They decreased the reliance on human labour and dramatically increased productivity and efficiency. The first water mills now began to appear in Britain.[7] One of the earliest tide mills, the remains of which have been unearthed on the banks of the Fleet in London, is thought to be of Roman origin.[8] It was built on a commercial scale and could operate several grinding stones simultaneously. Such mills allowed the production of wheat and barley to increase to levels hitherto unknown. During excavations of the Walbrook river, which in earlier times ran through the centre of London, houses and shops were uncovered including a bakery and later a large, circular brick-lined oven. Strong evidence in the form of bits of machinery, fragments of quern-stones and huge quantities of burnt wheat suggests that a mill also existed on the Walbrook and was possibly two or three storeys high. The grain was likely to have been brought, by barge, up from the Thames onto the Walbrook on the top of the tide and unloaded at the mill.

The Bakers

Though we know little about London's early bakers themselves, it is highly probable that most bread making and baking was carried out on a commercial rather than a domestic scale from the start. The miraculous survival of buildings and artifacts at Pompeii provides insight into the sort of lifestyle the Romans would have brought to Britain and would certainly have been incorporated into the creation of new settlements such as London. Large bakeries and their mills were located on main streets and on riversides, their premises situated close to the grain supply. Commercial bakeries with their own mills, ovens and various labour-saving devices were the norm. Special kneading machines existed where the dough was wound around a horizontal shaft in the bottom of the basin, then pressed between wooden slats in the sides. Only the shaping of the loaf and the mark of the bakery was done by hand.[9]

These first bakeries open to the public provided London's population, civilian and military, their families and slaves, rich and poor alike, whether merchants, tradesmen, craftsmen, boatmen or sailors, with the means by which they could obtain their daily bread.

The real importance of the Roman conquest, which brought with it new ways of organizing society and more sophisticated technology, was that it speeded everything up, especially in the production of bread. By establishing centralized grain storage and building water mills, the immediate prospect of starvation as a result of crop failure was much reduced. The move away from subsistence towards a market economy was made when the concept of surplus was introduced. With commercial ovens, specialist bakers and the provision of outlets where it could be sold, the making of bread took its very first step on the road to industrialization.

Some Roman Bread Recipes

In Roman Britain, the indigenous population would surely have continued to eat the griddle breads they cooked beside their fires. It is open to question just how much bread, as we know it, was made on a daily basis, but a pre-Roman 'technology' certainly existed whereby a form of bread could have been baked in an enclosed space of some kind. An oven, even a simple clay container with tight-fitting lid, allowed the baking bread to retain some moisture which greatly improved its texture.

On the other hand, wheat grown in Britain then would have been the 'soft' type, low in protein and gluten compared with the grain grown in hotter climates. Baked in an oven, it would still have been coarse and have hardly risen, even had it been made with just wheat. The grain of the peasant would more than likely have been a mix of rye, barley and oats; the addition of dried peas and beans, mixed with water and heated, would have more easily provided the pottage upon which he generally survived. With an occasional supplement of meat, this has been the essential daily sustenance of the peasant and his family for many hundreds of years, and has hardly changed even up to the present day.

Much of what we know about the bread that Romans in Britain ate is largely based on our knowledge of life in Pompeii and in Rome. We do know that the Roman army in Britain baked their daily bread in the ovens they brought with them and that public bakeries flourished in the Roman Empire from as early as 300 BC. At the point the Romans invaded Britain there were known to be some three hundred specialist pastry chefs in Rome. We also know that the Romans enjoyed several kinds of bread: 'lentaculum', a flat, round loaf made from emmer (a cereal grain closely related to wheat flour); oyster bread (to be eaten with oysters); 'artolaganus' or cakebread; 'speusticus' or 'hurry bread'; tin bread; Parthian bread and the slipper loaf.[10]

The privileged and wealthy could afford to eat richer breads containing milk, eggs and butter. The Egyptian grammarian and philosopher Athenaeus, who lived in the third century AD, has provided us with considerable information about bread and baking in those days, writing that 'the best bakers were from Phoenicia or Lydia, and the best bread-makers from Cappadocia'. He listed the types of bread common in his time: leavened loaves, unleavened loaves, loaves made from the best wheat flour, loaves made from groats or rye, and some from acorns and millet. There were crusty loaves too, loaves baked on a hearth and bread mixed with cheese, but the favourite bread of the rich was always white bread made from wheat.[11]

It is clear that the Romans had sophisticated tastes; assuredly the invaders would have enjoyed similar breads and pastries once settled in Britain.

ROMAN SPELT SLIPPER BREAD

This recipe is one given on the excellent Doves Farm website and the title is based upon the recipe writing of the Roman scholar Apicius. A 'slipper' is a low rise loaf. This bread is made with a slightly wetter dough than many bread recipes and the resulting loaf has an appealing wheaty flavour and good crumb structure.

Ingredients:
500 g (1 lb) wholegrain spelt flour
½ teaspoon salt
1 teaspoon Quick Yeast
1 tablespoon honey
400 ml (2 cups) water
1 tablespoon olive oil

In a large bowl, mix together the flour, salt and yeast. Dissolve the honey in the water and roughly mix it into the flour. While the dough is still craggy add the oil and mix well. Pick up the sticky dough and throw it back into the bowl. Do this 100 times.

Cut the dough in half and drop the pieces onto a large oiled baking tray which has been dusted with flour. Dust the loaves with flour and gently form into an oval. Leave to rise in a warm place for about 25 minutes. Preheat oven to 200°C / 400°F / Gas 6. Bake for 30-35 minutes.

ROMAN STYLE TWIN LOAVES

This easy to make bread uses more liquid than many recipes, and with just one rising it bakes two loaves with an appealing crumpet-like crumb structure. Resist adding extra flour to the sticky dough. This is an ideal recipe for bread in a hurry, making one loaf to eat almost immediately and one for later.

Ingredients:
400 ml (2 cups) water
1 tablespoon honey
500 g (1 lb) organic wholemeal spelt flour
1 teaspoon Quick Yeast
½ teaspoon ground sea salt
1 tablespoon olive oil

Makes: 2 loaves
Equipment: 2 x 500 g / 1 lb bread tins, oiled

Warm the water and honey until dissolved then leave it to cool Put the flour, yeast and salt into a bowl and blend them together. Stir in the water and oil, mixing to a soft, sticky dough. Knead the dough in the bowl for 100 presses. Sprinkle a little flour over the dough and cut it in half. Shape the dough pieces to fit your tins. Place each dough into its tin, cover them with oiled cling film and leave them in a warm place to rise for 25 minutes.

Preheat the oven to 200°C / 400°F / Gas 6. Bake for 40-45 minutes. They are done when the bottom of the loaf sounds hollow when tapped. Leave to cool on a wire rack.

A ROMAN FLATBREAD: PIADINA

This ancient recipe has been adapted for modern day use. Piadina are thin, flat disks, chewier and firmer than bread. Originally they were cooked on an earthenware plate called a testo, which was placed over hot coals. Today, piadina can be made on the range top using a modern day cast iron griddle or a heavy well-seasoned cast iron pan.

Ingredients:
3 cups unbleached all-purpose flour
3 tablespoons lard
1 teaspoon extra virgin olive oil
1 teaspoon ground sea salt
1 ⅓ cups of water

Pour the flour on the work surface forming a well in the middle. Add the lard and knead the dough using just enough lukewarm salted water to obtain a rather firm dough. Knead vigorously for approximately 10 minutes. Allow the dough to rest for 15 to 20 minutes. Divide the dough in 6 equal pieces. Roll or stretch each piece of dough into a disk 8 inches in diameter. Riddle each disk with the tines of a fork.

Heat a heavy well-seasoned cast iron pan on the range top. Before cooking, test the pan by letting a few drops of cold water fall on it. The pan is ready when the water skips and sputters across its surface. (If the water just sits and boils, the pan is not yet hot enough.) Place one of the disks of dough in the pan. Let the disk heat well on one side and then turn it over. When little charred bubbles form on each side of the disk, the dough is ready. Cook each disk of dough in this manner, stacking the cooked piadina in a towel so that they stay warm.

Chapter Four

The Trading Thames

The occupation of the country after the Roman conquest led to a huge reshaping of the largely Celtic way of life that had prevailed previously. The change wrought by the Romans takes us out of prehistory and into a more recognizable world.

Though there is scant evidence of Romans using the upper and middle Thames for trade, it seems highly likely that they did. They already made extensive use of continental rivers for trade and communications, and inland barge traffic was a common feature. In southern England, where there were no roads running from east to west, the Thames would have presented itself as a natural highway. The second century Celtic barge loaded with ragstone from Kent, excavated at Blackfriars in 1962, shows that shallow draughted, flat-bottomed barges were in use.[1] There may well have been similar vessels plying their trade between London and the grain-producing settlements further west.

After the Romans left, the following centuries were indeed 'dark'; little is known about the daily lives of those who lived in Britain during this period. Waves of marauders from other parts of Europe, driven out of their own lands by others moving in and remote from civilizing Roman influences, descended upon Britain, slaughtering the inhabitants and forcing survivors to retreat to the west. Many were captured and became their conqueror's slaves. The old Roman centres of population were destroyed: the Anglo-Saxon invaders had little need of them. They came not as traders but as farmers, living in villages, cultivating their strips of land, turning fields which once grew wheat and barley for Romans into pastureland for their beasts. These new farmers were essentially swineherds and their pigs ran free in the forests. They slaughtered their animals at the end of each year, grew rye for their bread and barley for their ale.

As subsistence farmers looking to grow no more than was needed to feed their own community, they had little requirement for Roman roads and bridges. These fell into disrepair and in time became hardly more than tracks. Public buildings with their myriad of uses were abandoned. How long the vestiges of Roman religion, culture and political systems survived is unknown, but all appear to have eventually been swept aside by the new order. Certainly Anglo-Saxon culture and beliefs were significantly different from either those of the native Britons or those which had been imposed by the Romans.

Politically, a crude kind of feudalism was taking root. The vanquished Britons and Anglo-Saxon settlers became serfs or bondsmen. They provided the large labour pool needed to re-establish a productive agricultural economy. The social hierarchy in Anglo-Saxon England created a perfect solution to the two main needs at the time: an organized workforce whose duties were defined by their stations, and an army ready for battle with minimal preparation.

The period between the withdrawal of the Romans and the arrival of the Normans, looked at from this distance, appears to be a time of non-stop fighting for precedence amongst neighbouring kingdoms, with periodic collective forays to quell invading hordes of Norsemen and others. We can be sure though that for the most part the ordinary people continued to follow the age-old rites of subsistence farming. Daily life still centred around the need to grow enough food to sustain life. Much of Roman technology was lost or abandoned and with it, seemingly, the energy to change and innovate, extinguished by a heavier, slower and more orthodox Germanic hand.

The city of London was abandoned, though the port survived

as a mere shadow of its former self. It remained as a trading post, but without the customers for imported goods and with no desire in the country to produce more than was immediate to their needs to sell abroad, the port operated on a considerably reduced scale than in the past. Without a large city population to feed and no surplus to store for shipping abroad, the need to bring grain to the city from the surrounding hinterland ceased and with it, to a large extent, the production of grain itself.

London began to revive from the mid-seventh century onwards. Records support the continuity of London's existence, though now it was a newer settlement beyond the city walls, with inhabitants involved in the pursuit of trade even through the most troubled times. The city had its own bishop in 604, at which time the Venerable Bede writes that London was the 'metropolis' of the East Saxons and 'the mart of many nations resorting to it by sea and land'.[2] The foreign trade of the port was stimulated by the seafaring and enterprising qualities of the new settlers.

Over the next three hundred years London was beset by constant Viking raids, which one might have expected to extinguish foreign trade, but the city was well fortified with strong walls, and sufficiently far inland to present great difficulties to the invader. It still remained the safest store place and market in the country and withstood many attacks. Moreover, the menace gave an impetus to the building of fighting ships which one assumes might have been used as trading vessels during periods of calm; more importantly, it meant that a shipbuilding industry was maintained. This in turn would lead to the development of increasingly sophisticated types of vessels. Evidence that London's trade continued, even during the disordered period which followed the death of King Alfred in 901, is found in a document of the latter end of the tenth century which records tolls chargeable at Billingsgate in respect of vessels from Normandy, France and Liège, as well as those of the Easterlings – the people of the Netherlands, the Baltic region and the Rhineland.

Once again, the settlement steadily grew back into a commercial and industrial centre and markets were created where none had been before. The old Roman city took on new importance as 'a centre of authority' and, as economic activity resumed, a port area known as Lundenwic was developed west of the city and the settlement itself started to expand northwards.[3] At the port's peak in the late eighth century, archeological assessments of the numbers living in London range between 5,000 to 10,000 people; not many to be sure, but considerably more than in any other settlement in England at the time. As an aside, it gives one pause when we consider the numbers we are talking about – in today's terms London's population then was no more than that of a large village today. Compared with the numbers thought to have lived there during Roman times – around 45,000 to 60,000 – its population in the tenth century is tiny. These figures do indeed put into perspective the type and size of communities we are looking at, not only in London itself, but also within the whole country. The plague, which ravaged all of Europe at various times from the seventh century onwards, would have also played its part in curbing the growth of population in cities.

London's primacy existed as much as anything because of its exceptionally large commercial hinterland, the core of which was formed by the valleys of the Thames and its tributaries. Christianity, by now well established throughout Britain, created a succession of minsters, churches attached to monasteries. Built close to the river, they stretched from Eynsham in Oxfordshire to the west, and eastwards to Barking and Tilbury on the estuary. For these religious houses the Thames was their highway and London almost certainly acted as an entrepôt, taking in monastic produce and sending imported luxury goods both upstream and downstream in exchange.[4]

As London's vitality grew, so the Thames also began to re-emerge as a route for trade and supply. A good example of this can be seen in the transport of salt from Droitwich in the Midlands. Even under the Romans, its salt was vigorously exploited, though production during the late Roman period is more doubtful. It was revived in the post-Roman centuries and on a substantial scale. The level of production indicates that it produced far more than was needed for local consumption and its markets went well beyond the immediate area. The kings of Mercia, in whose lands Droitwich was located, gained control of the region's most valuable resource. Their territories then extended as far as London. It was during this period that the many monasteries were founded, and though they were essentially religious houses their main function seems to have been as places of manufacture. The earliest of industrial entrepreneurs, the Church, promoted economic growth; the production of salt became organized and managed by both the royal manors and the monasteries. An increased need for salt stimulated production. The rise in demand came not only from London, where evidence points to the carrying out of large-scale butchering of cattle and of subsequent meat distribution, but from the Saxon population as a whole; salt to make brine was a vital commodity, allowing them to preserve the pig meat that sustained them through the winter months. The processing of hides in tanneries also added to the demand. Foreign merchants who were now trading in London regarded English salt as a valuable export commodity.

The great bulk of it would have been sold on the open market for onward trading by way of long established salt-routes. These routes, dating from far more ancient times, ran across the Severn to the west and northwest, but most led to the east and south over the Cotswold Hills and towards the line of the Thames. Two of these routes reached the Thames at Lechlade in Gloucestershire and at Bampton in Oxfordshire. Lechlade at the head of the navigable Thames was probably a place of special importance and may well have been where the transhipment of salt from wagon to small barge on its final leg of the journey took place. The major marketplace for the sale of salt was almost certainly London and its connections with the Droitwich-Worcester area during this early period are well evidenced. It was a profitable product, no doubt – both Church and Crown could levy taxes and demand tolls to be paid as it made its journey by land and water to the city.[5]

Salt, the history of which happens to be well documented, is an exemplar of how the rise of London and the Thames as a transport route go hand-in-hand. London and the Thames were again growing in significance, with Westminster the most important monastery in the land and the place where Saxon kings were crowned. Alfred and his successors ruled over a relatively peaceful country from their capital city until the coming of the Normans.

During William the Conqueror's reign the fortunes of London changed yet again. The Normans had little need for a capital city, or a permanent seat of government, since government took place and laws were made by an itinerant king and his court wherever they went. Though neither William nor his successors were based in one place, moving their courts between the various towns and palaces of their lands in England and Normandy, London, with its sea route to the Continent, was conveniently situated for a leader with an Anglo-Norman empire to rule. William would generally stay long enough to hold court at Westminster for the great feast of Whitsun when he would entertain his leading barons and clergy.[6]

Despite the conquest, life in the city continued much as before. Ships unloaded at Billingsgate, Dowgate and Garlickhythe, and the markets at Eastcheape and Westcheape were busy and noisy. Although most of the town's population, which numbered between 10,000 and 15,000, was still of Saxon origin, it was a cosmopolitan place where Normans, French, Norwegians, Danes, Jews, Germans and Flemings mingled.

As part of the Norman empire, with royal links to Flanders, and without serious threat of attack from Vikings, London's overseas trade flourished. New wharves were created along London's riverbank, as well as a new parallel road, the modern-day Upper and Lower Thames Streets.[7]

By the late Norman period, Westminster was considered one of the most important of the royal palaces. Over time, the business of ruling England was becoming more complex and the king needed to devolve duties to a growing bureaucracy. It was less convenient for his officials to be continually on the move, and a royal court with permanent offices was steadily becoming established. During the time of William II, the Court of Exchequer, responsible for the accounts of the Treasury, began to conduct its business from the Great Hall at Westminster, with its clerks housed close by. The head of the Exchequer, the Chancellor, was also responsible for the creation and maintenance of laws.

In the first half of the twelfth century, a new charter was granted to London by the king, marking an important early step in the city becoming self-governing and obtaining other freedoms.

By the middle of the twelfth century, London, abandoned after the Roman occupation and re-established by Alfred the Great, was once again England's major town and port, dominated by the Tower of London in its south-east corner and the vast St. Paul's Cathedral, newly finished in 1240, in its west. As the only dry crossing point of the Thames in the whole of the southeast of England, travellers found it more convenient to pass through the city than elsewhere. In 1176, after several successive wooden bridges had been destroyed by fire, Henry II commissioned the building of a permanent stone crossing. It took thirty-three years to complete and was to last for more than six hundred. It featured a central chapel, a host of shops and houses (the rent from which funded its construction and upkeep), gates, a drawbridge, waterwheels and a mill. It was 275 metres in length and supported on twenty Gothic arches. This later London Bridge formed a barrier across the river through which the largest seagoing ships could not easily pass; an additional incentive then to load and discharge at London. The creation of new wharves by the Norman riverside landowners, as well as the ever-increasing size of ships, was turning London into a major port.[8]

To feed this flourishing city was still the overriding priority and the Thames was steadily being reshaped to undertake this formidable task. A riverside community with the special skills needed to build larger ships, to handle such vessels and navigate the waterway, began to develop in earnest.

Early Medieval Bread

In a period when plague was a frequent visitor and poor weather could destroy harvests, great efforts were made to keep the price of bread low, to maintain good quality, and to prevent corruption and dishonesty. The mixing of dough and the baking of bread was, until relatively recent times, firmly within the domain of the professional baker. The law supported bakers in preserving their craft to themselves; guilds prevented unlicensed people from starting up; becoming a baker required an apprenticeship of seven years; and statutes were regularly published with various penalties for any infringements.

A common mix of wheat, barley and rye gave rise to the name of Maslin bread, from the French *miscelin*, meaning mixture. This mixed flour bread fed the lowest classes in medieval society, and was also used to make the bread plates called trenchers. For the privileged few, using the very finest wheat, Manchets, or Pandemain (Lord's Bread) was baked. However, bearing in mind that the stone milling and boulting methods of the time were unable to remove all of the bran from the ground wheat grain, even the best flour produced was an off-white colour. An authentic Maslin bread uses a sour dough starter while Manchet bread, using only pure, double sieved wheat flour, is made with a brewer's yeast. The following recipes are from the website of Oakden, the suppliers of bespoke griddles and bakestones.

MASLIN BREAD AND A TRENCHER

Maslin bread would have been round and domed shaped with a flat bottom and baked directly on a bakestone or the flat floor of a bread oven. The recipe below is just over a third of the size of a regular medieval loaf.

Ingredients:
200 g (7 oz) rye flour (traditional stoneground)
100 g (4 oz) barley flour (traditional stoneground)
350 g (11 oz) of stoneground wholemeal flour (plus extra for dusting)
500 ml (2 cups) of warm water (1 part boiling, 2 parts cold)
1 teaspoon ground sea salt

Raising Agent:
15 g of dried yeast & 1 teaspoon sugar (made up according to instructions below); or
30 g of fresh yeast & 1 teaspoon of sugar (made up according to instructions below); or
200 g (7 oz) of sourdough starter

The Trading Thames

Note on raising agents: In the medieval period (and for many thousands of years before) common breads made to feed the lower classes used an initial sourdough, 'fed' over several days, to start the necessary yeast cultures to make the bread rise. A live bread yeast (or other type) is fine for this recipe, particularly if you want to make it the same day, although by taking your time to make and use a sourdough starter this will give the bread a more intense and authentically rustic flavour.

Dried Yeast (if using dried yeast as a raising agent): In a small bowl or jug pour in half the warm water (250 ml), dissolve in the sugar, and sprinkle in the yeast, whisk it thoroughly. Leave to sit for 10 minutes in a warm place to allow the yeast to start to work. Check to see if the yeast is rising. After about 4 to 5 minutes it will have a creamy and slightly frothy appearance on top. Do not allow the yeast to sit longer than 12 minutes before using; leaving it too long will exhaust the yeast before it is in the dough. When ready, stir and pour in all the remaining warm water (250 ml).

Fresh Yeast: You need twice as much fresh yeast as dried yeast and you must use it in half the time after activating it. Make in exactly the same way as above.

Sift the flours into a large mixing bowl, sprinkle over the ground sea salt, mixing it well into the flour so it does not interfere with the yeast when it is added. Make a well in the centre of the flour. Add the yeast water (or just the warm water if using a sour dough starter). Bring together into a dough with a knife, wooden spoon, or your fingertips. If you are using a sourdough starter add it now, (don't mix in the sour dough until all the warm water is in and mixed with the main flour otherwise it tends to go lumpy).

Add some more wholemeal flour (if needed) until you form a firm dough which you can knead, it should still be on the 'sticky' side, but not so that it is difficult to remove from the bowl. It should be springy and elastic. Take the dough out of the bowl and place on a flat, floured work surface.

Knead the dough for about seven minutes (kneading dough is a 'push-pull' technique to break the gluten and starches down in the flour). If it sticks to the work surface sprinkle over a little extra flour from time to time but be careful not to overdo it. It is ready when it becomes satiny and when pressed with a fingertip the indentation in the dough rises back out.

Form the dough into a large ball, place it back in the bowl, cover with a light cloth and leave in a warm room until it has almost doubled in size – this could take up to two hours. If using a sourdough starter, make sure you give the bread much longer to almost double in size; it can take many hours depending on the temperature of the room.

Once the dough has almost doubled in size, knock it back, by punching the air out of the dough in the bowl. Remove the dough, knead once more on a work surface for one minute. (NB: it is at this stage that you could remove some dough mixture to keep to make into a sourdough starter for the next loaf of bread.) Shape the dough into a ball, place on a greased (with a little butter), non-stick baking tray, or into a loaf tin (see below). This can be one large ball, or several smaller ones to make individual rolls. Leave to rise once more for a further half an hour.

Preheat the oven to 230°C / 450°F / Gas 8.

At the end of the half hour, using a sharp knife, make a shallow cut all around the side at the bottom of the dough and cut a cross into the top. Place the oven tray into the preheated oven and bake for 10 minutes, then reduce the temperature to 200°C and cook for a further 40 minutes, or until the bread looks nicely browned and sounds hollow when tapped. Remove and leave to cool.[9]

MANCHET BREAD

There are several variations of this recipe. If you were able to afford it, the Manchet was the most common kind of bread eaten throughout the Middle Ages. Made with the best flour then available they develop a good crust and have a soft, dense crumb.

Ladie Graies Manchets (1594)

Take two peckes of fine flower, which must be twice boulted, if you will have your manchet verie faire: Then lay it in a place where ye doe use to lay your dowe for your bread, and make a litle hole in it, and put in that water as much leaven as a crab, or a pretie big apple, and as much white salt as will into an Egshell, and all to breake your leaven in the water, and put into your flower halfe a pinte of good Ale yeast, and so stir this liquor among a litle of your flower, so that ye must make it but thin at the first meeting, and then cover it with flowre, and if it be in the winter, ye must keepe it verie warm, and in summer it shall not need so much heate, for in the Winter it will not rise without warmeth.

Thus let it lie two howers and a halfe: then at the second opening take more liquor as ye thinke will serve to wet al the flower. Then put in a pinte and a halfe of good yest, and so all to breake it in short peeces, after yee have well laboured it, till it come to a smoothe paste, and be well ware at the second opening that yee put not in too much liquor sodenlie, for then it wil run, and if ye take a litle it will be stiffe, and after the second working it must lie a good quarter of an hower, and keep it warme: then take it up to the moulding board, and with as much speede as is possible to be made, moulde it up, and set it into the Oven, of one pecke of flower ye make ten caste of Manchets faire and good.[10]

Here is the recipe in more manageable amounts (a peck is 14 pounds) and written out in a user-friendly form for today's baker. It makes 6 to 8 rolls, two medium-sized loaves or one large loaf.

Ingredients:
¼ cup ale or beer lukewarm + lukewarm water to equal 2 cups
2 tablespoons of dry yeast
1 tablespoon ground sea salt
2 cups wholemeal flour
4 cups all-purpose flour

Mix the yeast and the ale together and add enough warm water to total two cupfuls in amount. Mix the two flours together and when the yeast has softened add the salt and stir in flour to form a dough. (NB: In this recipe one is stirring the flour into the liquid.) Add the flour carefully – it will probably need 4 ½ to 5 cups of flour to get the right consistency. Knead until it becomes elastic and the dough has formed. Cover and leave to rise until doubled in bulk – anything from an hour to two hours.

Turn out the dough onto a floured work surface and knead into a smooth ball. At this point you can divide it into loaves or rolls. Flatten the dough with the palm of the hand and make a ¼ inch deep slash all the way around the roll. Slash a decorative pattern on the top if you choose. Leave the bread to rise until doubled in bulk. This will take an hour or two.

Bake your bread in a preheated oven (230°C / 400°F / Gas 8) until the crust is golden brown. It should sound hollow when tapped on the bottom.

A SECOND MANCHET LOAF

Ingredients:
500 g (1 lb) plain white bread flour – unbleached stoneground (plus extra for dusting etc.)
200 g (7 oz) wholemeal bread flour – stoneground if possible and sieved,
or use 650 g (1lb 8 oz) of traditional 80 percent extraction plain stoneground white bread flour from an artisan miller, freshly ground if possible.
450 ml (2 cups) warm water
1 teaspoon ground sea salt

Raising Agent:
15 g of active dried yeast & 1 teaspoon natural brown sugar; or
30 g of fresh yeast & 1 teaspoon of natural brown sugar

If using active dried yeast, pour 225 ml of the warm water into a small bowl or jug, dissolve in the sugar, sprinkle in the yeast and stir thoroughly with a plastic or wooden spoon. Leave to sit for about 8 to 10 minutes in a warm place to allow the yeast to start to work. Check occasionally to see if the yeast is rising and frothing. After about 4 to 5 minutes it will have a creamy and slightly frothy appearance on top. When ready, stir and pour in the remaining 225 ml of warm water.

Do not allow the yeast (barm) to sit longer than 12 minutes before using; leaving it too long will exhaust the yeast before it is in the dough. If using fresh yeast it is necessary to use twice as much fresh yeast as dried. Make the fresh yeast barm in exactly the same way as the dried, but use it within 5 or 6 minutes after activating it.

After weighing them out, sieve both types of flours using a medium meshed sieve into a large mixing bowl. If using 650 g of an 80 percent extraction rate bread flour from an artisan miller it is not necessary to sieve the flour. Sprinkle in the ground sea salt, making sure that the ground sea salt is mixed in well with the flour so that it does not interfere with the yeast when added. Make a well in the centre of the flour.

Sieving the two flours will aerate the 500 g of white bread flour and sieve out about 50 g of the largest wholemeal bran particles from the 200 g of wholemeal flour – leaving about 650 g of usable flour in total. When the yeast is fully activated, pour the barm into the well in the flour, bringing the flour and water together into a dough with a wooden spoon.

Add more plain white bread flour, if necessary, until a firm dough is formed which is then kneaded. It should still be on the 'sticky' side, but not so that it is difficult to remove from the bowl. It should be springy and elastic. Take the dough out of the bowl and place on a flat, floured work surface.

Knead the dough for about 7 minutes. Kneading dough is a 'push-pull' technique to break the gluten and starches down in the flour.

Kneading Technique: Hold one end of the dough with one hand and then with the palm of your other hand push the dough away from you, stretching it out. Once stretched (without breaking the dough) pull the dough back in and over with your fingers into a bigger lump. Give the dough a quarter turn then repeat. Giving the dough a quarter turn before stretching it back out works all of the dough over the 7 minutes and stretches the gluten out in different directions. If it is sticking to the work surface or feels a little wet, sprinkle over extra flour from time to time during the kneading process, but do not over do it as too much additional flour will make the bread tough.

When it's ready it will become satiny and elastic, and when pressed with a fingertip, the indentation in the dough will rise back out. Form the dough into a large ball, place it back in the floured bowl, cover with a clean, light cloth and leave in a warm room until the bread dough has almost doubled in size – this could take up to 2 to 3 hours (depending on the temperature of the room).

After the dough has almost doubled in size, knock it back by punching it once to remove most of the air. Then gently knead it between your hands for a further two minutes. Shape the dough into a ball and place on a greased non-stick baking tray or a traditional bread baking stone. Leave to rise for a further 35 to 45 minutes; this is called the second rise.

Preheat the oven to 230°C / 450°F / Gas 8.

After the second rise use a sharp knife to cut a line into the top – not too deep or long, about 4 cm by 6 cm, and don't depress the dough too much when making it. Place the oven tray or baking stone into the preheated oven and bake for 10 minutes, then reduce the temperature to 200°C / 400°F / Gas 6, and cook for a further 40 minutes, or until the bread looks nicely browned and sounds hollow when tapped.

Remove the Manchet bread to a rack and leave to cool for an hour. Eat within 36 hours and keep the bread covered or in a bread tin.[11]

Chapter Five

The Making of Modern England

As with the Romans, the Normans' effect upon English governmental and social organization was profound, and although the daily life of the peasant farmer continued largely unchanged, the way it was controlled by those above him in status was something he would definitely have experienced.

The rather more sophisticated Anglo-Saxon form of medieval government that existed in England was handed over to the Normans. The aristocracy began to assume a much more important role. The pre-Norman landscape had already begun to change from that of isolated hamlets, moving towards the establishment of larger villages engaged in arable cultivation in a band running north-south across England. This reorganization of the English agrarian landscape, once achieved, remained much the same for the next several hundred years. Those who farmed grain, principally wheat and barley, were fixed at their appointed social station, only really rebelling when taxed so heavily that they were in danger of starving to death. In spite of internecine strife, changing weather patterns, plague and pestilence, the status quo mostly prevailed until the turmoil of the Industrial Revolution turned lives upside down in both the countryside and the town.

As the Church and the nobility became soundly established, and with the primary landowners largely taking control of the means of food production, the need once again arose for the land to provide more than just the daily requirements of those who farmed it. No longer simply the means to survival, food was rapidly becoming the basis of commerce, seen in terms of surpluses and profit to be exploited by an ever-rapacious Church and a greedy aristocracy. Farming had become a business, with the production of surplus essential to the creation of wealth.

Even so, it was only after long centuries of agrarian improvement and the opening up of international trade that dependence upon the state of the home harvest was substantially lessened. The harvest had always been at the very heart of the economy and its health was determined by the vagaries of the weather. The ordering and regulation of markets, controlling the flow of goods and ensuring a constant supply, steadily became the affair of government. Whilst in England the business of the marketplace was relatively free in comparison to other European states, the feeding of a population, many of whom were no longer in direct contact with the land, was of paramount importance and needed to be protected.

The twelfth and thirteenth centuries were periods of huge economic growth throughout the country. The population rose from approximately one and a half million in 1086 to four or five million in 1300. This growth stimulated increased agricultural output and the export of raw materials to Europe. By 1300, around 6,000 water mills of varying power and efficiency existed to grind corn into flour, and this freed up peasant labour for other more productive agricultural tasks. Granaries and tithe barns had become huge buildings, built to store enough grain year on year to feed the ever growing numbers.

Consider the daily requirement of just one man: records show that for a Benedictine monk in the Middle Ages the basic daily food allocation was a loaf of bread and a gallon of ale. A bushel of wheat in medieval times produced sufficient flour for twenty loaves of bread, and a bushel of barley enough malt for twenty gallons of ale. The low yields typical of this period meant that one acre of land grew about six bushels of wheat and seven bushels of barley. It follows that, with the three field system of arable farming adopted in southern England, to feed one man for a year about 8 acres of land was needed. A typical medieval farming village in England, of around 180 people, required some 3 square miles of arable farmland just to feed that small population, which is in keeping with the fact that such were villages typically located about 2-3 miles apart.[1] Give thought then to the amount of acreage required to grow enough grain sufficient to feed an urban population, particularly one as large as that of London.

Even though the country was still self-supporting in its supply of basic food commodities, the grain grown must be increasingly brought to London from further afield than its immediate surroundings, there to be stored in public granaries. The early English economy had finally ceased to be one of subsistence and more and more crops were being sent for sale to the towns. But the cost of holding grain for any length of time and the physical limitations on the size of granaries, along with the potential for total loss by fire or infestation by weevils and rodents, meant that storage was generally only sufficient to house the annual harvest. The possibility, therefore, of fairly immediate famine if the crop failed remained ever-present.

The expensive equipment needed for brewing and baking, particularly large bread ovens, created a commercial market for beer and bread. Until relatively recently, the baking of bread at home was never a feasible option in large towns. Professional bakers selling their products to the general public was the norm. With this level of commercialization came the need for regulation: the control of quality and pricing, and the checking of weights to avoid fraudulent activity by food providers. This most basic of grain-based food and drink, so central to people's lives, required authorities to ensure that even the poorest could afford them. People flocked to the city in search of a better life and charitable handouts. Henry III in 1244 made provision for 20,000 meals to be distributed to the poor in Westminster and 15,000 at St. Paul's. By 1300, London probably contained an even higher number of poverty-stricken inhabitants.[2]

In England, in 1266, the Assize of Bread and Ale was created. Its statute placed controls upon bakers and brewers by regulating the price, weight and quality of any bread and beer manufactured and sold in towns, villages and hamlets. The Assize set the price of ale and the weight for a loaf of bread costing one farthing (one quarter of a silver penny). Every year the Assize would set the size of a loaf according to the price of wheat and other grains – if it was in short supply and therefore expensive, one's farthing would only buy a small amount of bread; when it was plentiful the size of the loaf would increase.

This statute was the first law in British history to regulate the production and sale of food, and lasted in England for over five hundred years. By the thirteenth century, the growth of an extensive and efficient set of controls over the market for the largest and most important commodity in the economy can clearly be seen.

In a very real sense, the actual base economic unit of preindustrial society was not the monetary unit, but the bushel of grain. In 1303, the Assize of Weights and Measures in England decreed that 'an English penny shall weigh 32 grains of wheat dry and twenty pence make an ounce. Twelve ounces make a pound and a gallon of wine weighs eight pounds; eight gallons make a London bushel'. Thus it was that grains of wheat, even then, effectively remained the underlying measure, and all other weights and volumes were derived from this base unit; a pound of money was a pound weight of silver made up of 240 silver pennies.[3]

Historic references to particular weights and volumes of goods can be very confusing. Magna Carta, for instance, talks of the 'quarter of London', which was the national standard measure for wine, ale and grain. It was approximately 500 lbs or a quarter of a ton. A quarter equalled 8 bushels or 8 gallons, then understood to be a measure for both weight and volume: the grain gallon (also known as the half-peck) was the weight of 76,800 kernels of wheat; the ale gallon was the amount of ale filling an equivalent container; and the wine gallon weighed an equivalent amount to a full gallon of grain. In time, as weights and measures became standardized, one quarter equalled 28 lbs; four quarters equalled one hundredweight, and twenty hundredweights a ton. Three hundredweights made a sack.

Bread was commonly sold in medieval and Renaissance England as the gallon loaf (also called the half-peck loaf), which weighed 8 lbs and 11 oz. Later, including during the Victorian period, it was nearly always sold as the quartern loaf, which was made with exactly 3.5 lbs of wheaten flour and whose finished weight was approximately 4.33 lbs. Thus, two quartern loaves of finished bread weigh the same as the older and larger gallon loaf.[4]

Another later enactment compelled London bakers to make bread of such sizes and weights as could be sold at either four for a penny or two for a penny. Since the price of each loaf was fixed by law, it follows that its weight naturally varied as the price and availability of wheat rose or fell in value. The London baker could not sell his own bread anywhere but in the public markets where retail dealers, generally women, bought it at the rate of thirteen batches for the price of twelve. The bread was then sold from house to house by these women.

As demand for bread grew, so supply of grain increased. More land came into production and attention was focussed on how to get the produce to where it was wanted. The roads across Britain were much improved by the Norman form of government. For the king and his retinue – and indeed his army – being able to travel around the land was an essential element in the control of his subjects. The distances between each farming community and the need to move goods to market by more than just pack horse also played their part in improving routes.

It was, however, a slow and costly undertaking to travel by road, particularly if distances between farm and market were great. An average pack horse could carry about one eighth of a ton, a wagon around five eighths, whilst a barge on the river might easily load thirty tons or more. London was in a prime position, able to make use of its river for the transport of both freight and people.

By the 1300s, the bulk of grain needed to feed a burgeoning population was being brought to London by barge, via the Thames. Faversham to the east and Henley to the west were fast becoming important grain entrepôts serving the growing city, and more efficient vessels were being built to accommodate the loads of wheat and barley flowing in from both directions. Those who sought to send their produce to the city had a great incentive to make the waterway safer and more easily navigable.

The British population had grown to such an extent by the beginning of the fourteenth century that the countryside could provide enough food to feed itself with a surplus to sell only under the best of conditions. There was no longer any margin for crop failures or even harvest shortfalls. At the same time, the climate was undergoing a slight change, with cooler and wetter summers and earlier autumn storms. Conditions were no longer optimal for agriculture. These changes in the weather pattern marked the end of the prosperity that characterized the period from the eleventh to the thirteenth century. A sequence of crop failures in 1315, 1316 and 1321 caused famine throughout Europe, during which millions of people died. This disaster happened at the same time as an infectious and fatal cattle disease struck down sheep and oxen wholesale. Without crops or cattle, medieval man faced disaster.

In the spring of 1315, unusually heavy rain began to fall in much of Europe. It continued throughout the spring and summer and the temperatures remained cool. The grain could not ripen. Straw and hay for the animals could not be cut and dried, so there was nothing to feed the remaining livestock. The price of food began to rise, doubling in England between spring and midsummer. Salt, needed to cure and preserve meat, became difficult to obtain since curing by evaporation could not happen in wet weather. With scarcity came even higher prices, unaffordable by the simple peasant farmer. Famine continued until 1322 and the period was marked by extreme levels of crime, disease and mass death.

By the summer of 1317, the weather had returned to its normal pattern but the people of Europe were incapable of making a quick recovery. One important factor was the scarcity of grain available for use as seed corn. Although historians are still unsure of the validity of the figures, records of the time seem to indicate that a bushel of seed was needed to produce four bushels of wheat. At the height of the hunger in the late spring of 1317, starving people had eaten much of the grain normally set aside as seed, as well as many of their draught animals.

It was not until about 1325 that the food supply returned to a relatively normal state, and the population began to increase again. The countries of Europe were badly shaken. The death rate had been high, and even nobles and clergy had perished from hunger. The world now seemed a less stable and 'gentle' place than it had before the Great Famine.

During the next few years the European, and with it the British, economy slowly improved until agricultural and manufacturing production eventually reached pre-famine levels. This return to normalcy was suddenly and swiftly terminated in the year 1347 by a disaster even worse than the Great Famine.

In 1348 bubonic plague – the Black Death – reached the shores of England. By the autumn it had reached London, and by the summer of 1349 it covered the entire country, before dying down by December. Estimates of mortality of between 40 to 60 percent of the population are today widely accepted. England was still a predominantly rural and agrarian society; close to 90 percent of the population lived and worked in the countryside. Of the major cities, London was in a class of its own, with perhaps as many as 70,000 inhabitants.[5] When the plague reached the city in November, some 30,000 of the population succumbed within days, whilst many others fled.

Unlike the previous crisis where famine and its consequences took its slow and relentless toll upon the people, bubonic plague struck almost overnight, causing the swift death of over half the population. One consequence that medieval England couldn't possibly have been prepared for was its catastrophic impact on trade and the economy. With thousands dying and many more fleeing, in many cases there was no one left to tend the land or the crops, and no one either able or prepared to make or supply food and goods. The towns, including London, emptied, and as a result international trade plummeted in 1348 and 1349, and trading, commercial and financial networks disintegrated.

The enormous death rate caused land suddenly to become relatively plentiful, and manpower in much shorter supply.

Labourers, both skilled and unskilled, could charge more for their work and in the resulting competition to secure workers, wages were driven sharply upwards and the profits of landowners were eroded. The landowning classes chose to interpret this rise in wage levels as a sign of social upheaval and insubordination and reacted forcibly. In 1349, King Edward III passed the Ordinance of Labourers, fixing wages at pre-plague levels. The ordinance was reinforced by Parliament, which passed the Statute of Labourers in 1351. The labour laws were enforced with ruthless determination over the following decades.

These legislative actions proved largely ineffective at regulating the market, but the government's repressive measures caused a festering resentment. The pressures bearing down upon the workforce were contributing factors to the Peasants' Revolt of 1381 and resulted in their demand for a complete end to serfdom. Even though the rebellion was eventually suppressed, the social changes it promoted were already irreversible. By around 1400, the last vestige of the feudal economic order was disintegrating and serfdom became virtually extinct in England, to be replaced by a form of tenure of land known as copyhold. The countryside became dominated by estates organized as farms, frequently owned or rented by a new economic class: the landed gentry.

The nature of the economy changed to meet new social conditions. The virtual halving of the population in little more than a year meant the amount of land given over to the production of grain decreased substantially. Farmed land was turned over to pasture, which was much less labour-intensive. The rearing of sheep and cattle assumed a new importance and boosted the wool and tanning industries.

With the fall in population, landowners were no longer receiving income from rents and were forced instead to lease out their land to newcomers. Peasants benefited with increased options for employment and higher wages. Society became more mobile as labourers moved to accept work where they could command a good wage. In some cases, market towns disappeared or suffered severe decline, despite the economic boom in rural areas.

The Black Death profoundly altered the contours of settlement in the countryside. Catastrophic loss of population led to abandonment of less viable fields, contraction of existing settlements, the disappearance of some market towns and the wholesale desertion of villages – more than 1,300 vanished between 1350 and 1500.[6]

Nevertheless, the landlords' discomfort ultimately benefited the peasantry. From the last quarter of the fourteenth century onward, he gained from lower prices for foodstuffs and a greater purchasing power. The progressive disintegration of the manorial system and waning customary land tenure enabled the enterprising, ambitious peasant to lease or even buy property and become himself a substantial landed proprietor. The century and a half following the plague has been called a 'golden age' in which the most successful peasants became 'yeomen' – an intermediate class, lying somewhere between the gentry and the common workmen.

Freed from having to sell his own labour, holding a fixed copyhold lease and enjoying greater disposable income, the new yeoman farmer exploited his land exclusively for his personal benefit, and often indulged in leisure pursuits. It was with the formation of this class that the type of cooking – pies, puddings and roasts – which forms the basis of English cookery began to develop. Consumption of meat by England's humbler social strata rose substantially after the Black Death with a reduced need for lesser grains, though wheat continued to be in demand.

In the City of London, the effect of the plague resulted in the concentration of wealth, often substantial family fortunes, into fewer and frequently younger hands, a circumstance that, when coupled with lower prices for grain, left a greater per capita disposable income. This created a newly affluent group, the guild masters – men involved in a particular trade who had risen in status to the top of their profession – who exercised monopolies and controlled who gained entry to their guilds.[7]

The demographic shift caused by the Black Death opened the way for new economic growth. The size of the population in 1348 was effectively reduced to that of 1100. It has been noted that the Black Death, unlike other catastrophes, destroyed people but not property. The survivors were left with the whole of Europe's resources to exploit, resources which were far more substantial than they had been two and a half centuries earlier. In this environment, survivors also benefited from the technological and commercial skills developed during the subsequent period. Viewed from another perspective, though it was a cataclysmic event and retrenchment was inevitable, the Black Death did ultimately diminish economic impediments and open up new opportunities.

Demand for water transport on the Thames had increased steadily from 1189 to 1350 until the catastrophic weather conditions of the early 1300s brought death by starvation to millions, followed by bubonic plague, virtually halving the population. These human disasters were reflected in all walks of life, including the business of the river, and go some way to explaining why, for instance, the carriage of goods, the state of navigation and the way business was conducted, underwent so little change during the ensuing period. Trade, once burgeoning, slumped and then remained fairly static for at least the next hundred and fifty years, until growth began again in the sixteenth century.

Early Medieval Bread: Barley and Rye Breads
Little is known for sure about what bread Anglo-Saxon and Viking settlers actually ate. It is safe to assume that they brought their eating habits and cooking methods with them and so the following recipes essentially reflect the bread eaten in the Nordic countries around that time. It is a moot point as to how genuine such recipes might be – all have been adapted for the modern baker, this one by Carolyn Priest-Dorman.

UNLEAVENED BARLEY BUNS

Ingredients:
2 cups barley flour
4 cups wholemeal flour
1 ½ teaspoons salt
4 tablespoons vegetable oil

3 ½ cups boiling water

In a heavy pan, over a medium-low heat, turn the barley flour in a tablespoon of oil until it darkens to an off-white colour; it should not turn brown.

In a large bowl, mix the barley and wheat flours together with salt and the rest of the oil, rub in the oil with your fingers until it is of a uniform consistency. Add the boiling water all at once and stir quickly. Take out a lump of dough and work it between your hands until uniform, glossy and translucent. Repeat with the rest of the dough, then work it all together into one smooth lump.

Divide it into 24 smallish balls, and shape into bagels by poking a hole through them. Arrange on oiled sheets and leave overnight. They won't rise much, if at all. Bake in a hot oven (220°C / 450°F / Gas 8) for 20 minutes. Lower temperature to 200°C / 400°F / Gas 6 and cook until 'done', about another 45 to 60 minutes. They'll have hard, dark brown undersides. Allow to cool. They are slightly sweet and taste good with butter.[8]

AN ANGLO-SAXON LOAF

Yeast ingredients:
3 tablespoons hot water
½ tablespoon runny honey
¾ teaspoon dry yeast

Dry ingredients:
1 cup rye flour
1½ cups less 1 tablespoon of wholemeal flour, plus a little more wholemeal flour to scatter on kneading surface
1 or 2 tablespoons milled flax seed
1 ½ cups wheat bread flour
1½ teaspoons ground sea salt

Wet ingredients:
1 cup milk
½ cup boiling water

¼ cup butter, plus a little more butter for greasing the bowl &
baking sheet
Final Ingredient:
1 egg

(NB: 1 cup = 8 oz = 200 g.)

Stir together the yeast ingredients and allow the yeast to develop
until bubbly, about 10-15 minutes. While the yeast is developing,
mix together the dry ingredients in a large bowl. Combine boiling
water and the butter, mixing until the butter is melted. Add the
milk and then the yeast liquid. Slowly pour the wet ingredients into
the dry mix, stirring regularly until the liquid is absorbed. Add the
egg and continue to mix.

Place the dough on a floured surface and knead until the dough
holds its shape when left sitting. If the dough is too wet and won't
hold shape, or is too sticky, add a little more flour. Grease the inside
of a large bowl with butter. Put the dough in the bowl, cover with
a damp cloth, and leave in a warm place for one hour.

Place the dough to a floured surface, and cut into four pieces.
Shape each piece into rounds and place on a buttered baking sheet.
Leave the dough rounds to rise again for a half hour. Place baking
sheet in a preheated oven 200°C / 400°F / Gas 6, and bake for 35
to 40 minutes.

BARLEY BREAD

Ingredients:
1 tablespoon active dry yeast
2 teaspoons brown sugar divided into ½ teaspoon and 1½ teaspoon
1 cup water (warm)
2 cups barley flour
1 tablespoon vegetable oil
1 teaspoon ground sea salt
⅓ cup chick pea flour

Lightly oil a baking sheet with nonstick spray and set aside. Put the yeast in a small bowl with ½ a teaspoon of brown sugar and ½ a cup of warm water. Leave in a warm place to proof.

Put the remaining ½ cup of warm water into a large mixing bowl, add 1 cup of barley flour and mix vigorously. Add the remaining 1½ teaspoons of brown sugar, oil and salt and mix well. Pour in the softened yeast mixture and beat briskly, then add the bean flour and enough of the remaining barley flour to make a dough that can be kneaded.

Place the dough on a barley-floured work surface and knead until smooth and elastic. Shape into two round loaves and transfer to the prepared baking sheet. Slash the loaves diagonally across their tops. Allow to rise until doubled in bulk. Oil the tops lightly, if desired, for more crispness.

Bake in a preheated oven (180°C / 350°F / Gas 4) for an hour using middle rack of oven. Check for 'doneness' by tapping the bottom. Place on a wire rack to cool.

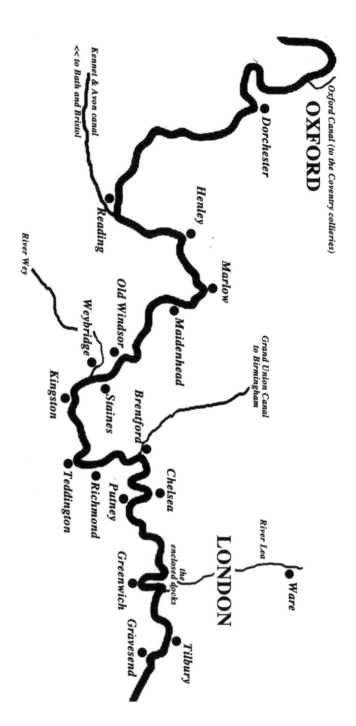

Map of the Thames, connecting canals and navigable tributaries

Chapter Six

The Developing River

A mere 215 miles (346 km) in length from source to mouth, the Thames, though modest in scale, has long been an established trade route, in all probability since the earliest man first built a raft or dugout canoe. The source of the river is about a mile north of the village of Kemble in Gloucestershire. From here, steadily receiving the combined waters of a number of lesser streams, the river flows gently through rich agricultural land to Oxford then to Reading, Henley-on-Thames, Marlow, Windsor, Staines and London. Today, the Thames enters what is known as Greater London just beyond Hampton Court. Nowadays the extent of its tidal reach is as far upstream as Teddington Lock, 20 miles above London Bridge and 55 miles from its mouth. Continuing on downstream beyond London, the river flows through flat low-lying lands to Tilbury, Gravesend and Canvey Island. The mouth of the Thames is at Yantlet Creek at Sheerness. Tides in the Thames estuary and English Channel rise and fall twice daily; it is this ebb and flow that has always greatly facilitated the passage of ships to and from London, especially in the days when they were sailed or rowed.

It is commonly held that the Thames is a navigable river and while this has always been generally true, it has never been necessarily so at all times and under all conditions. The Thames, like any other natural waterway has, over the centuries, had its course changed by floods, erosion, silting and the like. Altered weather patterns have frequently affected its navigability: prolonged warmth lowers water levels while colder weather causes stretches of the river to freeze. Seasonal weather conditions can lead to it overtopping its banks or diminishing to a mere trickle; too much water or too little and rivers become tricky things to navigate successfully. Man-made interference, such as the construction of bridges, weirs or embankments, changing the river's natural course by making 'cuts' to shorten distances or speed up flow, and the dredging of shallow stretches, has frequently made navigation more, rather than less, difficult.

In its more or less natural state the Thames once flowed much more slowly than it does today, and was a relatively easy river for barges to work. In Roman times, the rise and fall of the tide was little more than a metre at London and the highest tides reached all the way up to Staines in Middlesex. This was the case until the series of pound locks and weirs, which maintained the depth of water for navigation and reduced the danger of flooding, was extended over the tidal section down to Teddington (now part of Greater London) during the early part of the nineteenth century. Since then, the tidal part of the Thames has effectively ceased at Teddington lock. The waters running downstream from the source, aided by the contributions of its associated streams and tributaries, might surge into full spate after heavy or prolonged rain, making navigation hazardous, but once the rushing waters had flowed over the banks and spread out across the water meadows, the current would ease to a steadier pace.

Where the tide pushed up to meet the downward stream, the water would again simply spread out across the surrounding low lying land. Only when the tidal section of the river was thoroughly embanked, almost from end to end, tightly corseted by wharves and quays and piled edges, and the upper stream's water levels controlled by locks and weirs and managed by appointed authorities, can it be said the Thames was properly navigable on a daily basis from source to the sea.

It seems unlikely that any substantial craft loaded with produce could ever have made a completely uninterrupted journey along the whole length of the river in its unimproved natural state. Small craft and rafts have probably been used to move goods on and around the upper reaches of the Thames since the beginning of time. There is some evidence to show this to have been the case, though generally the ferrying about of goods was more likely at a local level, rather than longer voyages up and down the whole length of the river. Later, as the river's importance as a trading route grew and it became subject to man-made changes and improvements, it seems likely that regular supplies from higher up the river, destined for London and beyond, would have been brought by small boats to the point where uninterrupted navigation became more reliable. Here, smaller craft could be discharged and their freights loaded into larger barges to continue the journey down river. Physical and written evidence of how certain aspects of daily life on the waterway were conducted is very sparse, even when we move into a time when accounts were being kept and events recorded. In the period from 1189 to 1600 there are virtually no written records of the river journeys that must surely have been undertaken. It is unlikely that any barge or boatman would have kept a diary recording his daily round. This is true even to the present day, when most firsthand descriptions of river life are essentially attestations written to record the history of a dying industry.

From the earliest of times there have been many concerted attempts to improve the river for navigation. For instance at Abingdon, not far from Oxford, a short section of the river was of a higher gradient than the sections above and below. This meant that boats could not pass through during the dry season. To overcome the problem a new channel of some two kilometres (just over a mile) in length was dug around the year 1053. From this evidence, one assumes that navigation of the river that far upstream was sufficiently important to warrant the undertaking of such a large project. It would also seem to indicate that there were plenty of craft wanting to use the river and they could have been counted in their hundreds rather than in tens. We know that records show the river being used in 1205 between Oxford and London, though we have no idea for what size of vessel, or for what part of the year and under what conditions, the waterway between these two points was wholly navigable. In any event, in that year William, son of

Andrew, was granted 'freedom from toll and hindrance' for a ship navigating between the two places. In 1227, twelve tons of Gascony wine came by ship from Sandwich, on the river Stour in Kent, to London and from there transferred to a boat for transport to Windsor. Other examples of goods carried by barge and delivered to various Thames-side towns abound, and include brushwood for Windsor used for fuel, lead and tin from London to Reading, while shiploads of corn regularly made their way down to London. There is evidence of several man-made 'cuts' on the upper Thames all designed to aid the passage of barges around difficult parts of the river. It was certainly navigable, at least for some of the time, for the first 185 miles of its course throughout the thirteenth and fourteenth centuries.[1]

Though Magna Carta and succeeding statutes stated that all the rivers of England were to be kept free for the use of vessels, the statute essentially enshrined a public right of navigation which already existed as a 'natural' right long before there were any written records. Though such matters seem of little importance in modern times, the ways in which certain undertakings could be carried out and by whom were often predicated on such unwritten rights. To be annotated in an official document usually meant that conflicts had arisen and incorporating them into written law was essentially to remove any doubt. Thus the barge master on the Thames had his rights of passage confirmed by Magna Carta in 1215.

Wealthy landowners might, and indeed often did, build obstructions across rivers in the form of weirs in order to pen or trap fish, or to provide a head of water to drive the wheels of the mills they owned. Those who challenged them, like merchants and carriers, might be of lesser status and therefore without the same political power. Nevertheless, in theory, if someone wished to use a river, then Magna Carta – and later other laws enshrining the right of navigation – demanded that such obstructions be removed, or at least any built since the reign of Edward I.

For centuries arguments over river use have been the subject of numerous recorded disputes, turning up frequently in various courts of law, tribunals and the minutes of meetings of navigation and port authorities. It has to be assumed that rivers, 'from time immemorial', had been freely used for fishing and navigation. On waterways with sufficient depth and flow, such as can be found on the Continent, floating mills were a common feature, though they were moored in the river outside of the main channel so as not to obstruct passing traffic. On the smaller, slower flowing rivers of England the floating mill was never a feasible option. Instead, the fixed water mill, which relied upon a channel of fast flowing water, became a crucial feature of the landscape. Before the arrival of wind-powered mills in the twelfth century, the water mill would have been the most important of all medieval industrial constructions. Its simple technology and general applicability has assured its survival for some eleven hundred years. By the late eleventh century there were more than 6,000 water mills in England. By the sixteenth, water was the most important source of motive power in all of Europe and by the nineteenth century there were probably around 20,000 water mills in England alone.[2]

When built on minor tributaries or unnavigable stretches of water it is unlikely that major disputes would have occurred. However, from the time of the Norman conquest and the rise of the feudal system, another unwritten law – that of 'Soke Rights' – required everyone to have their corn ground in the mill of their manorial lord. Although the 'Right of Soke' was never written into law, it was commonly practiced in Britain – and throughout Europe – until the sixteenth century and in some places until as late as the nineteenth.[3] As land became increasingly privatized and the manorial system strengthened, the building of mills with their associated weirs increased. A mill-building landowner would want to construct his mill in places where he could take advantage of a natural and strong flow of water, the very same places where craft might choose to navigate. With an ever growing population to feed and improvements in farming techniques which enabled farmers to produce greater quantities of grain than ever before, the number of mills multiplied and increasingly were being built on established navigations or on rivers with potential for improved navigation.

It was not until 1579 that the first known survey of the Thames between Maidenhead and Oxford was made. Here it is stated that there were 23 flash locks, 16 mills, 16 flood gates and seven weirs between these two places. Seven of the flash locks were not attached to an attendant mill and were probably at fishing weirs or specially erected to take barges over particularly shallow stretches of river. In 1580 one John Bishop, almost certainly a corn merchant or barge owner, complained to the Lord Treasurer that the locks and weirs were causing considerable havoc to barge traffic. He says that many flash locks were so increased in height that 'Some of these Locks were extraordinary dangerous in passing. The going up the Locks were so steep, that every Year Cables had been broken that cost 400*l.* and Bargemen and Goods drowned. And in coming down, the Waters fell so high, that it sunk the Vessels, and destroyed Corn and Malt wherewith they were laden'.[4]

He was answered in a petition from those 'concerned in these locks and weirs and mills',[5] giving their reasons for retaining the flash locks. They said that the mills were close to the particular towns and villages for whom the corn was ground; the lock through the weir was necessary for the passing of barges and if weirs were removed the stones and chalk and rubbish from which they were built would choke up the river. Furthermore, the cause of the increased peril was that 'Barges were become of greater burthen; almost double what they used to be', and that the bargemen loaded them beyond reason. They refused to tranship their cargoes at the weir and reload them after passing through, as they used to do. Now they would unload nothing. Added to which, 'they employed people of no skill; they travelled so late & so early as to be unable to see what they were doing…it was no wonder the cables parted; they were made of ill stuff, and the barges so great and so heavily laden'.

Such conflicts between millers and bargemen continued. Both parties had need of the water: in the case of the boatman, he needed enough depth to be able to move his loaded craft without running aground or falling foul of underwater obstructions; the miller needed a sufficient head of water to provide the motive power to grind his corn. Mills worked best where the gradient of the river bed sloped sufficiently to allow the water to flow fast enough to turn the

Early Thames flash lock.

mill wheel. This natural flow could vary considerably depending upon the weather. By building a weir, which was effectively a wall across the river, and thereby holding back the flow, the water level could be raised substantially. The impounded water could then be diverted to the mill by way of a constructed stream. This was the mill-race, where the speed of the flowing water was increased sufficiently to turn the wheel. Above the wheel, the stream was known as the headrace; below it, the tailrace, which channelled the water back into the main river below the weir. By building up the water level above the weir and only allowing controlled amounts to flow past the wheel, the river level below would become shallower. The water from the tailrace spillway tended to create scours and sandbanks where it flowed back into the main river, thus making navigation more difficult and dangerous. Water flowing over the weir would have the same effect, requiring the river to be dredged at regular intervals.

For the man in a boat, a weir was not in itself a bad thing. Weirs help to make rivers navigable by raising water levels; the problem was how to get these boats past the dam-like constructions. Part weirs and split weirs with wide gaps presented less of a problem.

However some of the earliest structures erected by mill owners were fixed, a solid wall of stakes filled in with chalk and stones, and made no allowance for the water flow or for passing barges. Such fixed barriers, which held back the water and created a buildup, also led to disputes with landowners whose fields became flooded as a result.

Increasing river traffic dictated that where weirs could impede navigation, they needed to be furnished with a central span some ten to twenty feet wide with removable tackle known as paddles and rhymers. When required, the paddles could be drawn to allow boats and barges to pass through. These openings became known as 'flashes' and were difficult and dangerous to use. When the tackle was removed, the impounded water would flow through the space in the weir at a great rate, building up the level below. Once the difference in levels above and below the weir was not too great a vessel mounting the stream could be hauled through by means of a rope attached to a winch positioned above the weir, aided by gangs of men and in later times, horses. For craft heading downstream, the rush of water would propel it through the gap and beyond, the crew steering and using barge poles to keep it moving and in the channel. This time the winch could be employed by attaching a line between it and the stern of the barge, so that its speed down through the flash could be controlled. The lines used were long and heavy and once worn could part under the strain, leaving the loaded boat at the mercy of the rushing water.

Even then the boatman's troubles might not be over. It often happened that a second mill lower down would intervene by diverting the welcome flow of water to his own wheel, robbing the hapless barge of the water it needed and leaving it stranded in midstream. The miller, for his part, resented the huge amount of water required to keep barge traffic moving. The level of the upper pound would drop by several inches each time the flash lock was used. It could often be days before the head of water he needed to turn his mill wheel would be built up again.

It is not surprising, therefore, that acrimonious arguments arose with all parties believing they had right on their side. At the same time, a necessary symbiosis existed between the transporters of grain and flour, and the millers who needed a steady supply of their raw material and the means to deliver the finished product; the requirements of both parties had to be addressed. In 1350 Parliament passed its first Act against obstructions to the highway that was the Thames. This and subsequent Acts led to the appointment of various commissions charged with carrying out the works required to ensure the river remained a navigation channel. From our own vantage point, it is easy to see how, for some three hundred years and in spite of all the numerous Acts of Parliament passed to deal with the problem, the variously affected parties, which included land and mill owners, fishermen, riverside communities, corn merchants, boatmen and barge owners, were almost continuously at odds with each other and all intent upon protecting their various interests.

Landowners and mill owners required by the statutes to allow the passage of craft through their weirs had to maintain the flash lock and supply men to operate it. For this a fee was exacted; the amount charged and the frequency and speed that the flash would be operated were all matters in the hands of the private owners and a source of great anger and frustration to the bargemen. In spite of all the enactments and the numerous commissions appointed, little appears to have been done to ensure continuous and uninterrupted navigation until 1623 when the first pound locks were built between Oxford and Clifton Hampden.

The invention of the modern pound lock, incorporating built-in vertical sluices with mitred gates at each end, is credited to Leonardo da Vinci, with the first lock of this type being built in Italy in 1495. More than seventy years later the first of these new locks appeared in England, though not initially on the Thames which, despite being the most important trade route in Britain, had to wait another sixty years before it saw its first pound lock. The installing of pound locks, which brought deliverance to both bargeman and miller, finally came about with the River Improvement Act of 1624 which authorized three locks below Oxford at Iffley, Sandford Mills and on the Swift Ditch at Abingdon. Now at last barges could pass easily from one level of impounded water to the next. To the relief of the

Early Thames pound lock.

miller, the extreme drop in water levels caused by the flash lock was ended. However it was still to take nearly another hundred and fifty years, to 1771, before any more pound locks were installed; the very last flash lock on the Thames continued in use until 1937.

Traffic continued to grow and the improvements to the river for navigation could barely keep pace. The river needed a dredged channel and deviations constructed, and the old riverside path, which was used by gangs of men employed to haul the craft along and which passed through private land and so was also subject to tolls, had to be kept in some sort of state of repair.

The towing of barges was performed by teams of men, their numbers ranging from five or six, though sometimes as many as eighty were needed to pull a heavy barge through difficult stretches of water in times of flood. Each team worked a particular stretch. The 'haler' (the word is thought to be a corruption of 'hauler') must contend with dragging a heavily loaded vessel along, often against a strong flow of water. Eyewitness accounts describe how each man

The Developing River

Two 'halers' towing a barge upstream.

in the tow wore a leather breaststrap, which was attached to the tow rope. These tow lines were up to 220 yards in length and weighed a quarter of a ton. So harsh was the use they were put to they could be almost totally worn out after just three voyages between London and Oxford. The line was attached high up on the mast to keep the enormously heavy rope clear of the water and obstructions like the osier beds over which it had to pass.

Sometimes, in their efforts to haul the barge along, the halers leaned so far forward they almost lay on the ground. A man was employed to tell them when to pull and when to ease off. Before horses were employed for towage, the riverside path was narrow, mostly unmade, often deep in mud and sometimes underwater, another occupational hazard for those engaged in this work, where it was easy to slip and fall or be forced to wade through freezing flood water. Consequently, towing barges resulted in frequent accidents and sometimes even drowning.

The expansion of the English economy in the twelfth and

thirteenth centuries has been linked to the growth in the use of horses for haulage. Draught horses bred for their pulling power were initially maintained for carting alone. It is perhaps a moot point why horses did not take over the hauling of barges much sooner than they did, and why men continued to do the towing until well into the seventeenth century.

As the amount of freight carried on the Thames rose, so did the number of men seeking this kind of work. Casual labour was always easy to come by and the steady enclosures of land left many destitute without the means to grow food for themselves. They were a rough and often desperate people and their presence in large gangs at various points along the river bank was intimidating; one imagines that they would have fought hard to ensure that their employment as haulers continued for as long as possible. Indeed for the most part there would have been no merit in employing horses to do the work that these men were already available to do. Their decline must largely be put down to changes in river management and the ability to control its flow, along with the growth in trade. However, without the eventual introduction of horses to provide towage for the increasingly large and heavily laden barges, long distance river and later canal transport would have been difficult, if not impossible.

By the 1730s, towing with horses was beginning to replace the halers, though the numbers required for each stretch of the river varied enormously. It was reported that a 128-ton barge needed only one horse for the downstream journey but between eight and fourteen when towing in the upstream direction. Horses, like the halers, were available for hire en route, with bargemasters making advance arrangements for regular passages. The business of horse haulage must have been substantial, with fodder and stabling, plus other ancillary services, required at regular intervals en route. A man must still be employed to lead the animals along the towpath. Lines would need to be dropped to pass other craft, and horses led across bridges or loaded onto ferry boats when the towpath changed sides. On difficult stretches of water, or when the river was in flood, it would have been the job of the haler to ensure the safety of his animals. On the other hand, records show that so

Several horses towing a pair of barges upstream.

considerable was the number of men put out of work as a result of the use of horses, that an Act of 1771 stated that they could apply for relief to the Thames Commissioners, who might authorize a payment of up to 4 shillings a week.[6]

Bargemen themselves abounded, and as rivers were improved for navigation more and more goods were being carried. While some manors used carts to haul their goods to market, others used them to integrate with the water transport network. It is likely there was sufficient trade on the Thames to maintain a professional class of bargemen, many of whom were individual owners of large craft, plying for hire up and down the river, supplying long distance water transport.

Trade grew and demand for certain commodities increased the quantities of cargo to be carried and therefore the size of the boats. It would take centuries before efficient mechanized means for loading and unloading craft would be developed; products like grain must be manhandled from their source, bagged and weighed, then carried on the backs of men to and from the granaries where they were stored and later stowed in barges for delivery.

The arrival of a cargo of grain by river was subject to a variety of regulations. The City claimed the right to measure the corn and this duty could only be performed by men known as corn-meters, who were appointed by a committee of the Corporation of London. The vessel must be unloaded by 'fellowship' porters appointed by the Alderman of Billingsgate ward. They had a prescriptive right to the porterage of all corn and other goods coming into the Port of London. Crews of ships and barges were not permitted to undertake this duty.[7] These men were the forerunners of the dockers and the business of porterage is a good example of how, in the times prior to the Industrial Revolution, every type of employment was governed by certain privileges and monopolies. Grain has always been a specialized cargo rarely mixed with other goods. This was a freight which must be kept dry and handled with care; not such an easy undertaking when boats were made of wood, and often leaked badly.

Transhipment between barge and shore on arrival in London was also a crude business. Normally the boats would just be beached on the river foreshore and the loading and unloading done by hand overside. Loaded craft, even when afloat, were often unable to tie against a wharf to discharge direct to the shore. In this case, it needed gangplanks running from boat to bank for men to move along with the sacks of grain upon their backs. Where they lay further out in the river's stream, lighters were rowed out to unload them and bring the goods to the shore. Sacks of grain, each weighing two and a quarter hundredweight, might have to be manhandled across the decks of several ships before they could be deposited in the lighter that would ferry them to the shore. Generally corn and grain from eastern England arrived in sacks; foreign grain in loose bulk. The quantity brought by any vessel could vary from between 200 quarters to 3,000. Thirty-seven and a half bushels of wheat, or four quarters and five and a half bushels, weighed a ton. The cargo of even quite a small barge could belong to as many as twenty different farmers.[8]

When the ship was ready to unload, the meter and his team of seven or eight porters would go on board. Two of the men would dip their shovels into the grain and the meter would fill his bushel measure. One of the porters would pass his strike, a flat rod, across the top of the bushel measure, 'striking off' any heaped grain. A sack was held open and the bushel of grain poured in; it was then hauled up out of the boat's hold by the other porters and shot into the lighter whose lightermen would ferry the grain to the quay. From there it had to be conveyed to the granary, where it was once again measured and carried in sacks to the floor of the granary to be stored, when it was again shot loose. The meter and his gang could weigh and remove as many as 400 quarters of wheat per day. When the grain arrived in sacks it was measured at a rate of 70 sacks (35 quarters) an hour. To accomplish this, the meter and his men had to be extremely agile and very strong.[9]

It is hard today, living in a world where machines operated by the push of a button do the lifting and shifting of thousands of tons of freight, to imagine both the physical strength and stamina that such work entailed, and the urgent ant-like activity of the hundreds of men employed to load and unload the ships and barges which crowded onto an increasingly busy waterway.

A BASIC PEASANT BREAD

This bread takes time to make. Begin the evening before with soaking the split peas and make the dough first thing the following day. It will need about eight hours in total to prove so will not be ready to bake until late in the afternoon.

100 g (4 oz) dried yellow split peas
200 g (8 oz) lively sourdough starter
450 g (1 lb) stoneground wholegrain flour
50 g (2 oz) pea flour
10 g (sprinkle) dried seaweed or ground sea salt
350 ml (1½ cups) water

Wash the split peas and place them in a medium-sized bowl. Cover with water and leave overnight to soak. Take the sourdough starter out of the fridge and leave overnight to get to room temperature. Next morning, mix together the starter, flours, seaweed (or salt) and water until a thick wet dough forms. Leave, covered, in the bowl for three hours or more. Meanwhile, drain and dry split peas. Coarsely chop them and set aside.

Turn the dough out onto a floured board, adding extra flour so that a workable dough forms. Steadily knead in the chopped split peas and form the whole into a loaf. Make sure the sides of the banneton are well coated to prevent sticking. Place the loaf-shaped dough into a cloth-lined container such as a banneton, the interior well coated with flour to prevent sticking, and leave to rise for at least four hours.

Place a large baking tray in the oven and heat oven to its highest setting (around 230°C / 450°F / Gas 8). Once it is hot enough, remove the tray, sprinkle with more wholemeal flour and turn loaf out of the banneton onto the tray. Score the top of the loaf with a sharp knife and bake in the oven for 25 about minutes. Turn out on a wire rack to cool.

Chapter Seven

Grain to London from the West

Feeding a city required great effort by pre-industrial societies. London's need for two essential commodities, grain and timber – wheat for bread, barley for beer, and wood for heating – continued unabated. It has been calculated that by the mid-fourteenth century, before the city was decimated by famine and the Black Death, the population of London was around 80,000 people. To feed this many people required perhaps an average of some 165,000 quarters of grain each year; of this total some 110,000 quarters came by water, with 55,000 quarters shipped annually down river from the western side of London.[1] Although the number of inhabitants dropped to around 50,000 after the Black Death, the subsequent rise in living standards created an increased demand for grain, thus the amount of grain consumed did not vary much from that of the pre-plague period.

In medieval times most cities, including London, relied on the surrounding countryside to supply basic foodstuffs. Not that it was the ready availability of food to feed the people which caused London to grow, rather it was because its political and commercial status intensified and its mounting wealth and importance attracted all classes of people to its gates. Yet without a regular supply of staple foods an urban population could not survive. There was a need to develop more efficient and productive farming methods and a transport network which could connect to areas further afield as they became part of the city's food supply.

Transport over longer distances by water was invariably cheaper and easier than by road. Bulk cargoes, such as grain and timber, were typically carried by boat where possible and by the 1300s certain waterside towns were becoming the repositories for such bulk goods. It seems likely that grain grown in the surrounding hinterland was brought to these places by water in smaller craft or in wagons where roads were serviceable enough. Here it could be stored and sold under regulated conditions. Heavier or bulkier freights were then loaded onto larger barges generally known as 'shouts' to complete the journey to London.

By the mid-thirteenth century Henley-on-Thames, a town situated on the boundaries of three English counties, Oxfordshire, Berkshire and Buckinghamshire, emerged as the highest point of effective navigation on the Thames. Above Henley, navigation had become increasingly difficult and uneconomical for larger vessels and although vestiges of trade struggled on, it was finally ended by the mid-fifteenth century economic depression. Henley was to become the last place to which heavy commercial barge traffic could navigate on a regular basis for the next two hundred years. Even so, it should not be assumed that the journey down river below Henley was in itself particularly easy. Between Henley and London there were at least five major mill weirs for a loaded barge to negotiate.

Located on the banks of the river some 65 miles or so upstream of medieval London, Henley is a prime example of how riverside entrepôt towns developed. From small beginnings in the trading of grain there arose a supply system based on granaries located at key assembly points, of which Henley was one, and in the places where the product was consumed. Specialist London-based middlemen, called cornmongers, began to appear on the scene. Their presence signified a change from the previous straightforward buying and selling process, which normally took place publicly in the market square.

These cornmongers arranged bulk purchases, often buying direct from the producers, treating grain as a commodity to be sold on to city merchants at the highest price. London merchants were

Poling a barge downstream at Henley.

widely recognized as regular visitors to Henley and the town is the only place outside London where London cornmongers are known to have owned granaries; for them it was clearly a major market and collecting point for grain.

By the later Middle Ages the Guild of Cornmongers had become directly involved in the regulation of Henley's market and fairs, although infringements of the Assizes of Bread and Ale, and forestalling offences (buying up goods in advance) were handled in the manor courts. In 1441 the burgesses of Henley elected two tasters of all victuals sold in the town – an early form of quality control. In the later fifteenth and early sixteenth century the guild, clearly concerned to restrict grain trading to the public market alone, issued ordinances requiring grain to be deposited there before it was sold.[2]

An ordinance of 1517 affirmed that between Michaelmas (29 September) and the Annunciation (25 March) the sub-bailiff would ring the market bell at noon, and in the other half of the year at 11 a.m. Any corn-buyer entering the market before these times could be imprisoned at the behest of the warden and twelve burgesses. An ordinance made soon afterwards required corn-buyers to pay a commonly agreed price, and to refrain from intoxicating the sellers in order to obtain lower prices, or from buying wheat beforehand in the countryside.[3]

In the early seventeenth century the town corporation remained concerned to enforce open trading during specified market times, which suggests that trading could have been taking place outside the market. In 1608-09 and 1625 it ordered that no grain was to be bought before the market bell had been rung.

Regulation of the market in this way is revealing and demonstrates the existence of a lively commercial centre full of transactions and negotiations, complete, it would seem, with the usual collection of wide boys, sharks and makers of the quick buck. Henley now functioned as a trading port and a transhipment point for goods carried between London and places beyond the Chilterns, supplying London with grain and wood in particular. Wine and other goods, sent from London and bound for Oxford, were offloaded here to complete their journey by road. Its riverside wharves could accommodate the smaller craft bringing harvested grain to the town from places further upstream. Once unloaded, sacks of grain were stored in large granaries owned by city merchants, later to be sent on down river in larger barges to Queenhithe in the Pool of London.

Records show the wharf at Queenhithe to have been in use in 1253, though it is likely that it was far older. The name 'queen' is thought to be a corruption of the word 'quorn' meaning 'corn' while 'hithe' means 'landing place' or 'wharf'. It was here that grain coming from the western reaches of the river was traditionally unloaded and distributed. Much of Henley's medieval wealth was based on this waterborne grain trade, which, until the Black Death, was dominated by London-based merchants operating there on a vast scale.

London's influence over Henley was at its most intense between the 1290s and the Black Death, when the population reached its medieval peak and numerous London cornmongers and fishmongers had established bases there. After the Black Death, which caused a huge drop in the numbers inhabiting London, the pattern of grain-exporting from Henley altered. London merchants were far less involved in the control of grain and its shipment to the capital. Instead, businessmen based in Henley acquired the granaries and the town changed from being a place subservient to the London market and the demands of its grain merchants to a smaller, rather more conventional town, which arranged and exported its own produce and that of the surrounding countryside.

By 1500 London had shrunk to around 40,000 to 50,000 inhabitants. Not only were there fewer people but they were consuming less pottage and bread and more ale and meat. In spite of this, Henley's importance as an entrepôt supplying London's needs did not greatly diminish. Rather it responded to an increased demand for barley to brew ale, as well as the desire for more wheat, which was steadily replacing the more common maslin, a mix of wheat and rye that was normally used in the making of bread for the poor.

These demands reflected the increased wealth of London's population; dependence on pottage and coarse bread had diminished while the consumption of ale, white bread and meat grew.

By the 1560s Henley was again a major supplier of London's grain with a concomitant growth in river trade and increased employment for the resident bargemen. Records show a substantial number of boatmen based in the town and many who owned shares in large barges which they plied for hire. It must be assumed that the freight business, particularly the carriage of both wheat and barley, was a profitable one.

Improvements in river navigation above Henley from at least 1560 meant that other Thames-side towns were beginning to compete for business and also to tranship goods. In 1635 the river was reopened to Oxford and beyond for larger barges. London's expansion during the same period meant that the impact of the competition upon Henley's trade was probably outweighed in the longer run by the increasing amount of exports from the surrounding countryside. Oxford itself had also become a place of some importance and needed its own supply of foodstuffs, including substantial amounts of wheat, barley and rye.

Though turnpike roads existed, journeys by laden carts pulled by oxen or horses were slow and often difficult. The cost of moving small quantities of bulk items like grain was considerable in comparison to river rates, particularly when more than a few miles was involved. The craft used could vary considerably in size and therefore the tonnage they could carry. The barges that plied the river above London had, over the centuries, developed into a distinctive type and became known as 'western barges'.

Evidence of dimensions of medieval inland craft is sparse, but it seems likely that barges of anything between 60 to 90 feet in length and with a beam of 10 to 14 feet were the norm. By the seventeenth century the biggest barges had become substantially bigger; some were nearly 130 feet long with a beam of 18½ feet, and able to carry 180 tons of cargo. From the mid-1700s all craft were required to have some means of identification painted on the hull showing their place of origin and tonnage. When laden it was ordered they must have a draught of no more than four feet. This last regulation seems to have been regularly flouted with bargemasters eager to cram in as much freight as the vessel would take.[4]

A barge of approximately 60 feet x 12 feet x 4.5 feet could comfortably load as much as 50 tons of bagged grain – around 500 quarters. Again, roughly speaking, this bulk freight would fill all the available hold space and the barge would sit deep in the water, drawing about 3 feet. It is possible that the very largest craft, those 130 feet long, may have been built, at least initially, not so much to increase the amount carried per se but to spread the weight of the cargo over a larger area so that the barge had a shallower draught.

Given the hazards of the waterway it is likely that lighter loads would have been the norm, though there is much on record concerning the way bargemen overloaded their craft to such an extent that huge buildups of water were needed to allow them to shoot the weirs via the flash locks. Their deep draughts then caused them to run aground in the navigable channel in the reach below, causing considerable holdups to the rest of the traffic.

The livelihood of any number of people was dependent upon the movement of boats and barges up and down the river. From the boatbuilders located on the riverbanks close to London, to the many hands required to load and unload the craft, to the casual labourers employed to haul them along. The barge itself might have a crew of up to six, including a helmsman who was assisted by bargemen armed with ash poles anything from 14 to 19 feet in length, which they used to keep the craft within the navigable channel.[5] Then there were those who charged tolls and fees, both for the men on a towpath that passed through private land and for the passage of the barge; there were the payments made to bridge keepers whose bridges the barge must pass under, and to those who controlled the flash locks at weirs, and later the pound locks that replaced them.

Though generally profitable, life for a bargeman was a hazardous occupation. Not only was he dependent on the vicissitudes of weather and water levels, wind, current and tide, but he was also always at risk, a potential victim of accidents caused by ice, snow and fog. He was obliged to steer his vessel through man-made works, weirs and bridges, which were often constructed with little consideration for their effect upon those working the river. He worked long hours, standing outside on deck and steering his laden barge with his heavy tiller. Even where it might be possible to hoist a primitive sail to catch whatever wind there might be to aid his passage, the whole contraption of mast and sail must be lowered for each of the numerous bridges spanning the upper river. To take full advantage of the tide, the current, and the flow of the water, required skillful handling of his barge and an extensive knowledge of all the hazards present up and down the river. A loaded boat would rarely be able to stop and tie up close to the bank for the night but had to anchor in the stream and a lookout kept for other craft. The crew's accommodation was beneath a crude canvas cover stretched over hoops at the stern of the barge.

Journey times between London and Henley before the complete modernization of navigation remained conditional upon weather and water conditions. Generally the upstream passage could take around three to four days, though in exceptionally bad conditions it might take as long as two or three weeks. Compare this with today's almost effortless trip in either direction, the journey between London and Henley, a distance of some 65 miles by boat, can be managed quite comfortably in a couple of short days.

The sight of London Bridge, one of the most prominent structures in medieval London, as it hove into view was probably greeted with some relief by the bargemaster and his crew. The stone bridge was a busy thoroughfare lined with shops and private houses. Beneath, the arches housed waterwheels used to power water pumps and corn mills. It was less of a bridge than a causeway with culverts. Its piers blocked 45 percent of the river's flow at high tide and even more than that when the water level dropped below the buttresses, known as 'starlings', which protected the pillars upon which the bridge rested.[6]

As the bridge aged the size of the starlings was increased, to the point that by the eighteenth century only a fifth of the river could pass unobstructed through the bridge at low tide. Thus the sluggish flow would act to slow the approaching barge and allow the crew to make the final manoeuvres needed to row or punt the vessel into the wharf at Queenhithe, or to drop anchor and unload into the lighters which would ferry the sacks of grain to the shore.

London Bridge acted as a constraint upon the shipping in the river and the wharves that they might work to. The quays at Billingsgate and Dowgate, situated below the bridge, were able to deal with much larger ships and barges coming upriver. It was to these quays that foreign shipping came.

During the eleventh, twelfth and thirteenth centuries other hithes and wharves were established along London's waterfront to handle a whole range of goods. Foreshores were flattened and chalk surfaces laid down, embankments were constructed allowing ships to berth close to the shore, methods of loading and unloading improved, as well as the wharfinger's storage facilities. As a result, the size of craft and the tonnage they could carry also steadily increased.

Queenhithe, above London Bridge, is usually regarded as the main destination for the grain transported down river during the Middle Ages. Here was a public deepwater wharf with an attendant marketplace for the sale of corn, fish and salt. It was busy enough for the harbour to be considerably enlarged in 1471 and was one of the four traditional markets (the others were Billingsgate, Newgate and Gracechurch) where grain could be sold in London. Concern for the continuity of the city's grain supply was reflected in the strict regulations governing how business could be conducted in the marketplace.

Again, as at Henley, ordinances were issued at various times and their aim was to ensure that the market in grain was an open one and accessible to the ordinary people of the city who could buy what they required in small quantities. This regulation was to make certain that it was not exclusive to wholesale dealers who would resell at higher prices. Other regulations, in place essentially to ensure that all the grain sold would go to ordinary citizens and to bakers and brewers, included the following:

– All market transactions were confined to three days: Monday, Wednesday and Saturday.

– No one was to meet carriers bringing goods by water or land in order to purchase before they reached the market.
– No cornmonger was to buy grain in the market in order to sell it again at a profit. Anyone dealing in grain must only buy it in other counties if they wished to sell it on in the market.[7]

It was further ordered that every new mayor must take oath to oversee the sale of victuals, enforce the assize of weight and measures, and punish abuses.

Parliament itself was concerned with the problem of high prices. It was the Commons that succeeded in getting the king to impose a prohibition on the export of grain and malt when the merchants of London and elsewhere were shipping so much out of the country that it was in short supply in the home markets and prices were being driven up. Later proclamations denounced 'forestallers' who bought grain in order to withhold it from the market to push up the price. Commissions were established in the relevant counties and authorized to summon jurors to 'discover the names of those involved in these corrupt practices and arrest them'.[8]

The involvement of kings and parliament with the control of the food market, supply and prices, sprang not so much from concern for the everyday welfare of ordinary citizens but more from the knowledge that when serious grain shortages occurred, which they did with some regularity, starvation caused people to riot, and worse. High death rates disrupted the life of the kingdom and the crown's ability both to raise taxes and recruit able bodies for the constant wars and military excursions that marked the passage of the Middle Ages.

Bread Made with Ale

The connection between the growing of grain and the brewing of alcohol is well substantiated. What is often overlooked is the link between brewing and the lightness of the bread consumed. This type of bread was popular among monks; they brewed ale, a key ingredient in good bread making, and knew that barley was a good source of sustenance.

BARLEY BEER BREAD

Ingredients:
500 g (1 lb 2 oz) barley flour
500 g (1 lb 2 oz) stone-ground wheat flour
1 teaspoon salt
250 g (9 oz) butter
beer to mix

Mix the flours and salt together and rub in the butter. Add enough beer to make a soft dough and shape into small cakes. Cook on a hot stone (or griddle), 5 minutes each side, until firm.

ANOTHER BEER AND BARLEY LOAF

200 g (8 oz) barley flour
400 g (1 lb) strong wholemeal flour
1 teaspoon ground sea salt
15 g (½ oz) fresh yeast
2 teaspoons clear honey
⅓ cup brown ale
2 cups warm water

Blend the yeast with a little of the ale to create a creamy paste, then add the rest of the ale, honey and 1½ cups of the warm water, mixing well. Mix the flour and salt together. Make a well in the centre. Add the liquid to the flour and salt, and mix until you have a firm dough. Add a little extra water if necessary to get the right consistency. Shape the dough into a ball, leave in the bowl and cover with clingfilm. Place the bowl of dough in a warm area of the kitchen and wait until the dough has risen to about twice its original size.

Remove the clingfilm, press the dough down firmly and split into two halves. Place each half of the dough in a bread or cake tin (depending upon the shape of loaf you want to bake). Cover each tin with a cloth and set to one side to allow the dough to rise further. Bake in a preheated oven (230°C / 450°F / Gas 8) for about 20 minutes. Remove from the oven and turn out the loaves onto a wire rack. Leave until cold before cutting and serving.

Chapter Eight

The Plague and the Fire

In 1509 London had a population of some 60,000. By 1650, with a population of about 350,000 it dwarfed all other English cities, and abroad only Paris and Constantinople were bigger. With the centre of the church at Southwark, and that of the crown at Westminster, with commerce in the City, the religious, financial and political hearts of the country were no longer separate entities surrounded by pasture and woodland. The huge increase in the population meant that they had become no more than wards within this heaving city of humanity.

Government had become centralized, with Westminster the permanent seat of power. London's port provided both an easy access to the markets of the Continent and a thriving economy controlled by the City and the guilds which operated within it. The dissolution of the monasteries in 1536 had furnished the wealthy of London with any number of fine buildings to live in and to conduct their business in, as well as providing stone from those demolished to build others. The land released – vegetable gardens, orchards and fields for livestock – was rapidly colonized by the poorer inhabitants and a huge number of dwellings, mostly constructed from wood, sprung up, erected in a haphazard and piecemeal fashion beyond the city walls.

Though a new reservoir at Islington, completed in 1609, fed a network of elm pipes laid under the major streets and some 30,000 houses were connected to the mains, the water itself was not of good enough quality to drink.[1] The brewing of ale was still vital in providing a safe means of drinking water and the demand for malted barley continued to rise.

The ability to feed this number of inhabitants on a daily basis was becoming stretched to the limit. Grain remained, as always, the main constituent of people's diet, primarily in the shape of bread, porridge or pottage, ale and beer. Though wheat, rye, barley and oats poured into London by water and by road, from the western reaches of the Thames and the east coast ports, as well as along the improved navigation of the River Lea, there was always an underlying fear that just a few poor harvests could upset the steady supply; shortage of bread and rising prices inevitably led to civil unrest and to the possibility of the poor starving.

Medieval London had never previously stored its grain in any long term way; the marketplace simply acted as the conduit through which grain passed from those who owned it to those who used it: the millers, bakers, and ordinary people wishing to buy what they needed in small quantities. Meal, a coarse ground flour, was also making an appearance in the marketplace. To be able to buy grain, ready ground, gave people a more direct access to the bread making process. The better off could make their dough at home and bring it to a local baker to bake. Families were becoming wealthier and could afford to use pure wheat instead of the maslin mix of wheat and rye, the usual diet of the poorer classes.

Unlike other staple products where price controls were set by various ordinances or royal decree, grain was normally left to find its own level. Some controls were in operation but their purpose was to give the townspeople, both rich and poor, every possible advantage in the purchase of corn coming into London. The City, in the Middle Ages, did not much concern itself with how it obtained its corn, but rather how it was to be disposed of. It was the point of sale rather than the supply that was the subject of regulation. The method was simple – the owner, countryman or urban dealer placed his open sacks in the marketplace and standing before them, waited for someone to buy. This could be anyone; a poor consumer, the servant from a wealthy household or an industrial employer, a miller or a baker. Although the price of a loaf of bread was fixed in relation to the price of corn, the grain itself was left to find its natural price in the marketplace. The actual sale price of the finished goods, whether a gallon of ale or a loaf of bread, was regulated by the Assize.

Unfortunately bad harvests were not uncommon and memories of the populace reduced to eating chestnuts, acorns, roots and bark were vivid and recent. In 1586 and 1594, the common bakers were instructed to bake bread of rye, barley, peas and beans. In 1622, the feeding of peas and beans to sheep was ordered to cease 'because in time of dearth the same may serve the poorer sort to make bread of',[2] and at such times many of the quite well-to-do also had to resort to eating cheaper and less palatable bread.

As the size of the population escalated, the authorities became increasingly anxious to maintain a regular supply of grain to the marketplace, and some means of storage became essential. Granaries were built at Bridgehouse, Bridewell, Queenhithe and Leadenhall. Bridgehouse was at the southern end of London Bridge, close to the mills whose waterwheels were sited directly beneath the final arch and driven by the water of the Thames; Bridewell was on the Thames on the banks of the Fleet river; Queenhithe was located beside the Thames above London Bridge, a little further east than Bridewell; Leadenhall was in the centre of the city.[3]

Over time, various restrictions and measures were introduced: increased monitoring of bakers by the Assize of Bread; restrictions on imports and exports; prevention of hoarding; and the regulation of the brewery trade, the open grain market and the activities of certain middlemen. Throughout the period 1600-1640 the City of London, in conjunction with the livery companies, operated a system to provide corn in the form of ground meal to the poor. A proportion of the grain stored in granaries was set aside for them. Ultimately a committee was set up by the Court of Aldermen to oversee both the provision of grain to the granaries and the delivery of meal to the market place.[4]

Despite setting and agreeing rules of compliance, even in the 1570s there was rarely sufficient grain in store to fulfill the mayoral precepts. It may be that it was considered wasteful by the livery companies to hold large amounts of corn unused in unsuitable granaries, where it was subject to deterioration and wastage. Instead it was decided to keep just sufficient to supply the markets with meal as and when required. Their calculations were sometimes wrong and in 1631 a poor harvest for the second year running caused widespread social unrest.

The so-called 'western rising' of 1628 and 1631 involved many in protests against the Crown's plans to sell part of the royal forests of Dorset, Wiltshire and Gloucestershire to courtiers and speculators. At issue was the loss of common rights in the forests and adjacent lands scheduled for enclosure. These protests took place within the context of poor harvests in the years 1627 to 1629 and continued throughout 1631. At the same time the English cloth trade had slumped disastrously, creating an industrial depression which left many workers close to starvation. Rioters in the grain-producing counties were also protesting against the siphoning off of grain from rural areas to meet the growing demand of the city during a time of extreme shortage locally.

It was widely understood that poor harvests resulted from poor weather, but grain shortages were further exacerbated by profiteers, middlemen seeking extra financial gain through the practice of forestalling and engrossing; discontent became rife when the hungry poor saw grain being loaded onto ships for export. At the same time there was also a long and widely held tradition which believed enclosure to be the real cause of dearth. Enclosure was used to withdraw ground from tillage, raise the price of grain and increase, if not create, the risk of scarcity. All such factors, real or supposed, contributed to the violent behaviour of the time. Fear of public disorder and rioting made the authorities even more determined that a constant supply of grain should be maintained and could be brought in from further afield when needed. Thus when London suffered its next disastrous calamity, happily it did not include hunger and starvation.

In 1665 the last major epidemic of the bubonic plague to occur in England struck London. In the time it lasted it killed an estimated 100,000 people, while some 200,000 or more fled to the countryside. Within the walls of London was a city of some 448 acres. This area had become so densely populated that any decent form of hygiene was impossible. In the poorer parts were overcrowded tenements without any form of sanitation; open drains full of sewage, slops and refuse ran through the streets; the stench was overwhelming. An additional menace arose from coal, a fuel which was rapidly beginning to replace the ever diminishing timber supplies. Factories making soap, breweries and iron smelters belched forth choking black smoke, as did the 15,000 or so private houses, which now exclusively burned coal for heating and cooking.

Outside the city walls, shanty towns of wooden shacks without any form of sanitation had sprung up. These suburbs were home to the craftsmen and tradesmen who flocked to an already overcrowded city and by the mid-1600s some 250,000 people lived in them. As these areas become more crowded, they turned into rat-infested slums. It was here in the parish of St. Giles-in-the-Fields that the earliest cases of the disease presented themselves. Once the plague took hold it simply ravaged the population who had, unknowingly, provided the perfect breeding ground in which it could travel, spread and decimate the whole of London, both within its walls and without.

In 1665, the total population of London and its immediate environs was estimated to be some 450,000 people. During the few months the plague was rife, it killed at least 100,000, striking people down with shocking speed. There was little or no time to prepare for what was to come and the natural response, from those who could, was to flee before it.[5]

Trade and business completely dried up and the streets emptied of people, other than the death carts and dying victims. That large numbers did not also die from starvation was largely down to forethought on the part of the City fathers. They had arranged that a commission of one silver farthing be paid above the normal price for every quarter of grain landed in the port of London. This was quite a substantial sum, but even so it seems surprising that any amount of extra cash would persuade men to carry grain to a plague-ridden city, with all the obvious dangers this entailed. In spite of the earlier bad harvests, the country was still largely self-sufficient in homegrown grain and there was no obvious shortage at the time. The main concern and reason for the one farthing per quarter sweetener was to ensure that sufficient grain was obtained and brought into London to keep those who remained there fed.

How grain and meal were landed and distributed while the plague was raging is not easy to discover. As usual there is little documented evidence concerning people's daily lives. Most information on the subject is garnered from the writings of Daniel Defoe who in 1722 published a novel, *A Journal of the Plague Year*, which purported to be an eyewitness account of the plague during the summer of 1665. Defoe himself would have only been about five years old then, but he grew up in London in the period afterwards and no doubt much of what he writes was gathered firsthand from those old enough to have experienced the full horror and had survived to tell the tale.

His narrator in the novel describes how, having decided to stay rather than flee, he laid in a store of provisions – enough basics to last for several weeks. He was reasonably well-off and had an oven for baking. He bought two sacks of meal to make bread, and enough malted barley to brew several barrels of beer. He bought a quantity of salt butter and Cheshire cheese but no meat. This last, because the plague raged particularly violently amongst the butchers and the slaughterhouses nearby.

He writes that people needed to go out every so often to buy provisions, and that was when they were most likely to catch the plague. Poor people were not able to lay in stocks so must go to the market frequently to obtain their meal and other provisions. Markets were set up in specified areas, and suppliers of vegetables, dairy products and other foodstuffs brought their goods to them. These markets, it was decreed, were to take place on streets in the open countryside that led to the entrances of the city. Here they negotiated their sales by shouting out the prices to the customers who were ordered to keep their distance. Money was doused in a bowl of vinegar or submerged in a bucket of water to 'disinfect' the coins before they changed hands.[6] Defoe also notes that country carts were bringing in supplies of roots, beans and dried peas, as well as hay and straw. The roots and legumes would almost certainly have been for the making of pottage, which still remained that most basic and timeless food of the poor.

Emergency measures were put in place. It was ordered that the freedoms of the market should continue to be observed. On each market day the Lord Mayor, or one of his sheriffs, attended on horseback to see that their orders were executed and that the country people bringing their goods were shielded from harm. Bakers too were subject to particular controls; the master of the Baker's Company and his assistants were ordered to follow the directives of the mayor and to see that they were carried out. The Assize of Bread was set each week, subject to how much grain was available – the weight of the penny wheaten loaf, which at the start of the crisis stood at 10½ ounces, never weighed less than 9½ ounces, even at the very height of the disease. All the bakers were ordered to keep their ovens going constantly on pain of losing their privileges as Freemen of the City. As a result, bread was readily available and sold at its normal price and weight.

As the narrator's profession is to do with exporting goods, he is particularly interested in what was happening to shipping and the Thames. He points out that virtually all navigation had come to a stop with ships neither coming or going. The port was packed, both above and below London Bridge, with many ships and barges lying at anchor. Seamen were unemployed, as were all the tradesmen and workmen who depended upon the building of ships. All work had ceased and the men discharged. The river was without movement. Ferrymen and lightermen had nothing to do. The port had ceased to operate: customs officers, watermen, carmen, porters and the scores of labourers dependent upon it for their already precarious livelihood, all were dismissed and put out of work.

During a walk to Blackwall, our storyteller happens to meet a waterman who is living on his boat while his wife and children stay indoors in his house nearby. They communicate at a safe distance and the waterman explains that he goes each day out on his boat to find food for his family, rowing as far as Greenwich and sometimes to Woolwich in order to buy fresh meat, as these riverside villages were then part of the surrounding countryside and free of plague. He ties his boat well downriver on the Kentish side and calls at isolated farms where he is known to obtain 'fowls and eggs, and butter'. When he returns home he lays it and what little money he has on a large stone nearby and calls until his wife hears him. He then retreats back to his boat and she comes and takes the food and coins.

The narrator asks him how he comes by the money and the food, and the boatman explains: he points to the water where all along the river there are ships lying in ranks five to eight deep, moored on the buoys in the centre of the river while many others lie at anchor further downstream. All are shut up with the families of their owners and merchants living on board. He explains that he fetches provisions, carries letters and does anything else absolutely necessary for their welfare. The occupants need never step ashore and he, the boatman, delivers their requirements into the ship's tender which is drawn up alongside. Once he has placed the goods in the tender, he backs off with his boat and someone climbs down and takes them back on board. Each night he ties alongside and sleeps on his boat. Thus does he manage to continue to work and earn his wage whilst at the same time having no direct contact with any other person.

The whole of the river was filled with hundreds of ships waiting it out. Most had people on board and as long as they had provision enough they could survive very well. He also reports how the watermen and bargemen who worked above London Bridge were able to convey themselves and their families further upstream away from the plague centre. The boats were furnished with hay to sleep on and many made coverings using their sails as tents. The riversides were lined with craft of all kinds, and the people survived as long as they were able to subsist on anything they could get from the countryside around them. It is said that while local people were not prepared to receive them into their villages, many nevertheless bought food and left it for the boat dwellers at a safe distance from their habitation.[7]

Most importantly, the narrator notes that two trades carried

The Plague and the Fire

London before the Great Fire.

on by water continued during the whole period of the disease: the provision of coal and grain. Grain brought into London by road soon began to fail, but it continued unabated by water, from a number of different routes: from Yorkshire and Lancashire, via the port of Hull; from Lynn, Wells, Burnham and Yarmouth, all in the county of Norfolk; from the Medway; from the coastal ports of Kent and Essex; downriver from the Lea and upriver from as far away as Oxford. That the amount and constancy was so great was due to the prudence and conduct of the Lord Mayor. He ensured the safety of the masters and their crews. He arranged for the corn to be unloaded whenever required and for the cornfactors to organize the discharging of their vessels. The master and his crew did not leave their ships and barges, and any monies owing was carried on board and left on the deck in a pail of vinegar.

The bargemen coming into London almost certainly brought all their victuals with them and had no need to leave their craft while they were unloading. As soon as they were able, they would have left the quay and anchored out in the river, awaiting the tide that would carry them away from the noxious city and its deathly stench.

These specific insights offered by Daniel Defoe are particularly useful as they explain, almost at firsthand, why comparatively few of the river fraternity lost their lives to the plague. It was later said that Charles II granted a special dispensation to the bargemen, in recognition of their service in bringing grain into London and keeping the people fed during this dreadful time. Known to all on the river, even down to the present day, as the 'eastabout-westabout charter', it gave those who had brought the grain, and their successors, the freedom of the river for all time and the right to navigate without the aid of London-based lightermen. The granting of such a dispensation gives some insight into how employment on the river was controlled then and the power already vested in the Watermen and Lightermen's Company.

As early as 1514, an Act of Parliament regulating watermen, ferrymen and bargemen and the fares they could charge received Royal Assent from Henry VIII. In a further Act of 1555 the Company of Watermen was formed and directed to rule over the activities of all watermen and wherrymen between Gravesend and Windsor. Like our latter day London black cab drivers, the men responsible for rowing their customers up and down and from side to side of the river were keen to establish exclusive control over their particular services. This Act also allowed the Company to introduce apprenticeships of one year for those wishing to learn the skills of the waterman, while a further Act in 1603 extended that period of apprenticeship to seven years. Unlike the other City livery companies, the Company of Watermen not only came into being to protect the interests of those involved in the carrying of passengers, but also with the brief to bring its members and their activities under some sort of control, to put an end to what the Act of Parliament of 1566 called 'divers and many misfortunes and mischances, caused by evil and ignorant persons who robbed and spoiled [passengers] of their goods, and also drowned them'.[8]

With only one bridge across the river and congested roads which were frequently impassable, the Thames was the thoroughfare

The Plague and the Fire

Old London Bridge and the Pool of London.

through London upon which all transport depended. John Stow's *A Survey of London* (1598) estimated that there were some 40,000 men earning their living on and around the river.[9] Ferrymen and watermen plied their trade from the many steps which led down to the water's edge, carrying their passengers both up and downstream, and across the river. In 1700, the lightermen, whose craft conveyed freight between the anchored ships in the river and the wharves where the goods were handled, were also brought under the authority of the Company. With its influence stretching far up and down river, its members were often drawn from areas a considerable distance from the City of London. Though not a trades union in the modern sense, nevertheless over time, as organizations such as the Port of London Authority and the Thames Conservancy came into being, its control over all the local activity taking place in the river meant it could exert great pressure on behalf of its members. Its influence, though in many ways positive, also created something of a 'closed shop' with consequences for river trade down to the present day. Interestingly, the terms of the 'eastabout-westabout charter' are still recognized by those who work on the river, even if they aren't codified in law. This has proved a valuable concession even in modern times, allowing for grain to be moved around and through the port by barge without the need for extra labour in the form of lightermen and the additional costs involved.

On 2 September 1666, a fire which started in a baker's shop in Pudding Lane and burned for four days effectively brought the plague to an end, along with everything else.

It is hard to imagine the double effects of plague and then such a devastating fire had on London's hard-pressed inhabitants. Survivors, many of whom had already lived rough in the countryside for nearly a year, having returned to London in the belief that the plague had run its course, now found themselves forced to flee yet again. Both the weather – drought conditions and high winds that changed direction at a crucial moment – and politics, which led the Lord Mayor to refuse Charles II's offer of soldiers and other resources to fight the fire at source, contributed to its rapid escalation. The mayor would not allow the Royalist troops into the city and when finally Charles did take over command, the fire was raging out of control.[10]

By the time it was checked it had consumed 13,200 houses, 87 parish churches, St. Paul's Cathedral, and most of the buildings of the City authorities. It is estimated to have destroyed the homes of 70,000 of the city's 80,000 inhabitants. Until the rain came on 11 September, the ground was too hot to walk on. The fire had burned so fiercely that though the flames were doused, Samuel Pepys noticed ruins still smoking as late as February the following year. Nevertheless the City recovered quickly. The Exchequer moved to Greenwich; other government offices soon found temporary premises, while the shopkeepers in the Royal Exchange, the centre of commerce for London, moved to Gresham College and had reopened for business by December.[11]

Though the promised new city never quite materialized, certain public buildings and the Thames waterfront received special attention. The unending line of hovels which bordered the river

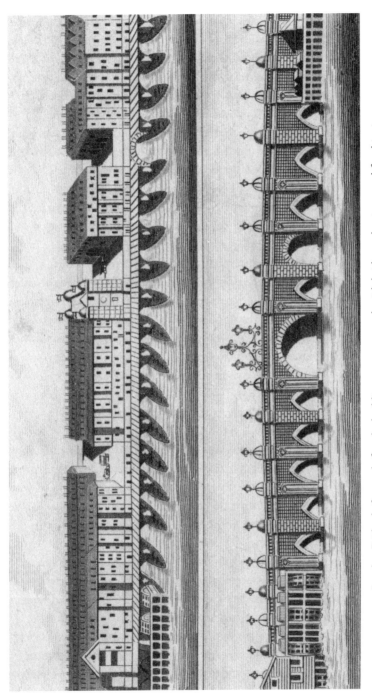

London Bridge before and after the buildings were removed, with bridge arches improved for shipping

bank to its very edge had made it almost impossible to use river water efficiently to extinguish burning buildings. Once these shacks were alight, the river became inaccessible both as an escape route and for firefighting. In the rebuilding of London it was decreed that new buildings must be set back by at least 40 feet from the riverside. A new quay was to be built stretching from Blackfriars to the Tower. Though the land was cleared and no new private houses were built, the area soon became obscured by cranes, sheds and warehouses. The desire for an open riverfront of public walks and gardens was quickly overwhelmed by the needs of trade, which was booming. Much of the material for rebuilding the city was brought in by barge, and space was needed to land quantities of stone, bricks and aggregate. Rebuilding went ahead at a remarkable rate.

Within the area of devastation, a new city solidly built in brick and stone arose. Though the destroyed district was but a small portion of the sprawling metropolis, it had become one of the most important centres of trade in the world. The opportunity to rebuild meant the creation a much more efficient City of London and, with its driving energy again harnessed, for it to become the very hub of the British Empire in the decades that followed.

BREDE AND RASTONS

Rastons are small round loaves made from sweetened bread dough with egg. After baking, the top was cut off and the crumb removed; the hollow shell was filled with finely chopped crumb mixed with butter, the top replaced and the whole served hot. Here is the original recipe, as given in the Harleian manuscript (MS 279):

> Take fayre Flowre and the whyte of Eyroun and the yolke, a lytel. Than take Warme Berme, and putte al thes to-gederys and bete hem to-gederys with thin hond tyl it be schort and thikke y-now, and caste Sugre y-now ther-to, and thenne lat reste a whyle. An kaste in a fayre place in the oven and late bake y-now. And then with a knyf cutte yt round a-bove in manner of a crowne, and kepe the crust that thou kyttest, and

than caste ther-in clarifiyd Boter and Mille the cromes and the botere to-gederes, and kevere it a-yen with the cruste that thou kyttest a-way. Than putte it in the ovyn ayen a lytil tyme and than take it out, and serve it forth.[12]

The following is an adaptation of Cindy Renfrow's modern translation, given in *Take a Thousand Eggs or More*, which includes actual temperatures, measurements, and modern ingredients:

2 tablespoons sugar
2 eggs beaten
1 cup warm ale or beer
1 packet of yeast*
3½ cups bread flour
½ cup butter clarified

*The ale yeast or 'barm' called for in this recipe is a solution of active yeast skimmed from working ale. Since modern, commercially available beer and ale are not active enough on their own, extra yeast has been added here.

Put 2 cups of flour and the yeast in a large mixing bowl. Add sugar, ale and eggs and stir well. Add enough additional flour to make a stiff dough. Turn out onto a floured board and knead until the dough is smooth and elastic. Form into a round loaf and place on a greased baking sheet. Cover and let rise in a warm place until doubled in bulk. (For a shiny finish brush the loaf with milk)

Bake in preheated oven (200°C / 400°F / Gas 6) for 25 to 30 minutes, or until the loaf sounds hollow when tapped. Remove the loaf from the oven and place it on a wire rack. When it has cooled completely, cut off the top crust and scoop out the center of the loaf. Cut the crumbs into pieces and mix with the clarified butter. Put the crumb mixture back into the loaf and cover with the top crust. Put the loaf in a warm oven for 10 minutes to heat the butter before serving. Remove from oven and serve hot.[13]

SAFFRON BREAD

This is a tasty medieval recipe adapted by Maxime de la Falaise in her compendious collection of Anglo-Saxon cookery, *Seven Centuries of English Cooking*:

Ingredients:
¾ cup milk
¼ teaspoon saffron
1 packet (½ oz) yeast
4 tablespoons lukewarm water
3½ cup flour
2 teaspoons salt
2 eggs
½ cup sugar (optional)
½ cup raisins (optional)

Scald the milk with the saffron and leave it to cool. Dissolve the yeast in the lukewarm water. Sift together 3 cups of the flour and the salt. Make a well in the centre of the flour, spoon in the eggs, milk, and yeast mixture and blend. (NB: If making the sweeter version add the sugar now.) Add enough flour to prevent it becoming sticky. Knead, adding more flour as needed, until the dough is smooth and elastic. Put in a greased bowl in a warmish place and leave to rise until it is double in bulk (about 45 minutes). Punch down and shape into a round loaf. Place on a greased baking sheet and leave to rise until again doubled in size.

Bake at 190°C / 375°F / Gas 5 for 25 to 30 minutes. Check for doneness by tapping the bottom of the loaf. Cool on a rack. (NB: If using raisins, knead them in after punching the dough down the first time. The sugar should be added to the eggs, milk and yeast mixture at the start of the process and mixed into the flour.)

This bread keeps well. It makes fine breadcrumb and if made without the addition of sugar and raisins is good for breading fish or veal.[14]

Chapter Nine

All Change

Recovering relatively quickly after the twin disasters of plague and fire, London continued its inexorable expansion. In the countryside changes of some magnitude were also taking place. As ever, the need to feed the people was the force transforming agriculture and reshaping the lives of those involved. The gradual changes to traditional farming in England that had begun slowly a century or two before began to accelerate in the eighteenth century. Particularly significant was the reallocation of land ownership. Having a more secure control over property allowed owners to experiment with ways to improve their yields. The farm became more compact and delineated. Farmers, better educated than in the past, were beginning to harness science to maximize their returns. They invested in technical improvements: new machinery, better drainage, new types and strains of grain, scientific soil management and improved systems of crop rotation.

Better management of the land, and the increasing use of horses and machinery that could do the work of several farm labourers, in combination with the land enclosures taking place, resulted in significant numbers of displaced countrymen and their families moving to the towns and cities in search of work.

Trade on the Thames burgeoned. This too was becoming more efficient and better organized. As the amount of work grew, so too did the size of the barge and the tonnage it carried. All manner of goods were being regularly transported by water between Oxford and London, and though other small upriver ports had developed and were trading just as busily, Henley continued to be an important entrepôt for supplies of malt, meal, grain and timber to London. Increasingly, it specialized in what became a major trade in the town: the malting of barley for use in ale and beer. New granaries for storage were being built in the 1780s, demonstrating ongoing expansion. Goods for local consumption also flowed upriver from London and beyond. Coal, in particular, was now of immense importance and increasingly used by local industries and in the home. Records show that loose coal was regularly landed at Henley, packed into sacks and then distributed by horse-drawn wagons.

In 1724, Daniel Defoe published a travelogue of journeys made during 1710 and 1720. As in his account of the course of the plague in London, Defoe is a useful raconteur of the day-to-day business being carried on at the time. He notes that at Marlow, a Thameside village in Buckinghamshire, where he stopped overnight, 'a very great quantity of malt and meal [is] brought hither from High Wycombe, which is one of the greatest corn markets on this side of England'. He also says that, 'Between High Wycombe and Marlow is a little river called the Lodden, on which there are a great many corn mills...[which] grind and dress the wheat, and then the meal is sent to Marlow, and put on board the barges for London'.[1]

In writing about Reading, Defoe described the types of goods being carried by the barges:

> Reading is a very large and wealthy town...Their chief trade is [by] river navigation to and from London...for the consumption of the goods which they bring by their barges ...particularly coals, salt, grocery wares, tobacco, oils and all heavy goods.
>
> They send from hence to London, by these barges, very great quantities of malt and meal, and these are the two principle articles of their loadings. Some of those barges are so large, that, I was told, they bring a thousand or twelve-hundred quarters of malt at a time; which according to the ordinary computation of tonnage in the freight of other vessels is from 100 to 120 ton.[2]

All Change

It seems clear that by the time Defoe was writing his travels, the practice of milling wheat destined for London some distance from the metropolis was a growing one, and mills situated on the Thames were beginning to send flour packed in sacks and barrels to the capital in their own barges.

Further downstream, the tidal Thames provided a reliable, constant and free source of water power, making London and its environs ideally suited for the construction of tide mills. This type of mill derives its power from the rise and fall of the tide. A dam with a sluice is constructed across a suitable tidal inlet. Seawater enters the pond through large sluices or 'sea gates' which open under pressure from the rising tide, and close automatically after high water. By opening the internal sluice gate, the pressure of the water from the mill pond can be controlled as it flows through one or more narrow channels, before hitting the paddle blades and setting the waterwheel and the milling machinery in motion.

The Domesday Book mentions, among others, Three Mills at the bottom end of the River Lea in Bromley-by-Bow. They operated as corn mills for centuries. In the 1530s, when Henry VIII dissolved the Stratford Langthorne Abbey which then owned the mills, they were still grinding flour for bakers who were celebrated for the quality of their bread and who supplied the huge City of London market of Stratford-at-Bow. By the eighteenth century, though reduced by then to two, they had become the largest tide mills in England with seven waterwheels, four in the House Mill and three in the Clock Mill. They drove fourteen pairs of millstones with an average weekly throughput of 125 tons. Over time, some 76 tide mills were recorded in London, including two on London Bridge. Further up the River Lea at Stratford were another eight or nine tide mills. Tidal mills were built at either end of the southern wall of the Tower of London where the moat discharged into the river. Remains of a tide mill have been found at Greenwich, and at various times, others at Stepney and Shadwell, Wapping, Old Ford, and the Crash mills between Whitechapel and St. Botolph Aldgate and at Bermondsey and Rotherhithe, are known to have existed. It is probably true to say that many such mills, whose history went unrecorded, their remains now buried under the massive port developments of later centuries, once stood isolated out on the Thames marshlands, reaping the double benefit of the waterway's tide-generated energy and making use of a navigation that brought the grain to its wharves and took away the finished product.

Though I have been largely writing about the movement of grain and meal to London from the higher reaches of the Thames, there was certainly as much, if not more, being sent by barge upriver from the counties bounded by the east coast and the Thames estuary, particularly from the county of Kent.

The farmers of northeast Kent possessed a number of competitive advantages, the most valuable being their proximity to major markets both local and in London. This region has long been a fertile crop-growing belt stretching from Rainham in the west to Thanet in the east. The region incorporates nearly half of the county's coastline, much of it bounding one side of the Thames estuary.

Transport by water of wheat, barley and its malt derivative, along with hops, fruit and vegetables, was the norm for the food market of Canterbury on the River Stour, the most important of all the local markets. Canterbury's prosperity rested in large part upon it being the chief commercial and marketing centre for the eastern half of Kent. The naval stations at Sheerness, Chatham, Dover and Deal were greatly dependent on regional supplies for at least some of their victuals.

The farmers of the region could perhaps have been content to simply satisfy local needs, but beyond these, and in competition with them, lay the ever voracious London maw. Its population had risen from 400,000 in 1650 to 675,000 by 1750, with a concomitant increase in the demand for foodstuffs. It was this demand that was largely responsible for the early commercialization of agriculture in northeast Kent. Wheat and barley were always particularly important crops, with the barley grown in the Thanet area the most highly valued and sought after.

The marketing of most agricultural products, whether they be fruit and vegetables, dairy produce or meat, rarely needed middlemen; the transaction took place between grower and buyer in a public market place. By contrast the marketing of corn – here used in the eighteenth century sense to mean wheat, barley, malt, oats, peas and beans – used indirect and complex methods, involving a high level of competition and speculation. These are bulk goods, durable in storage, which can be graded and standardized. The supply of corn can be subject to severe fluctuations – the weather, the state and amount of the harvest, transport and storage costs – while demand tends to be fairly constant.[3]

The marketing of corn, by its very nature, attracts middlemen; these are the traders, speculators, merchants and others engaged in making their money as the product moves from field, through the markets, to its final destination in the baker's kitchen or the miller's grain store. Kent attracted such men. Its acreage under wheat expanded rapidly during the 1700s and opportunists kept a careful eye on the fluctuating market, especially when wars with France and Spain made importation of foreign grain problematic. Unlike other agricultural products such as fruit, vegetables, dairy products and meat, whose short life and transitory nature largely precludes interference by third parties, grains and legumes could pass through several hands after harvesting before reaching their final destination.

These are bulk products that can be dried, graded and stored for protracted periods. Wheat and barley in particular are always in demand, but their supply and availability are subject to fluctuations caused by the weather, which affects both the amount and quality of the harvest. Nor do transport and storage costs remain constant. Once the grain was harvested the farmer would keep what he needed to feed himself and his family, selling his surplus on to specialized traders. At this point it is no longer just a food product per se, but becomes a 'commodity' which can be speculated on, traded with, invested in, and withheld from sale if necessary.

Dennis Baker's erudite essay concerning the marketing of corn in Kent in the eighteenth century provides insight into how this trade developed so rapidly into a sophisticated commodity market – largely because a viable transport route existed and craft were

A hoy disembarking passengers into rowing boat at Billingsgate.

developed to allow the rapid movement of bulk product from source to the City of London.

Corn, a word then used to denote a whole range of cereals and legumes, was despatched from the Kentish ports of Whitstable, Faversham, Herne and Thanet. Between them they supplied three-fifths of all of London's supply coming in from the seaward side of the city. As John Boys, a Kentish farmer writing in 1790, put it: 'The chief part of agricultural commerce of this county is that of exporting corn to the London Markets'.[4]

Until 1750, Queenhithe above London Bridge, and Bear Key below it, were London's two greatest specialist corn markets, probably comprising the greatest corn market in Europe at that time. It was to Bear Key that came 'all the vast quantity of corn that is brought to the city by sea, from the counties which lie commodious for that carriage',[5] as Daniel Defoe put it in *A Tour Thro' the Whole Island of Great Britain*.

Though the passage from the Kent ports to London was relatively short it could nevertheless be quite hazardous. Winds, tides and currents combined with the shallow waters of the North Sea to create tremendously rough and dangerous waters for small craft. The estuarial waters of both the Netherlands and England are very similar, and over time a small, strongly-built barge, flat bottomed, shallow drafted and equipped with leeboards and sail, evolved to cope with both the vicissitudes of the North Sea and the tiny tidal creeks where they would load their freights. Known as 'hoys' – the word is Dutch in origin – these sturdy barges were mostly owned by small farmers in both countries and were the means by which they could convey their produce to market.

The hoy had a distinctively rounded, slightly bulbous bow and protruding stempost, making it easy to identify in old paintings and prints where it is often depicted beached on a foreshore, unloading produce from its hold. A version of this vessel came to be particularly associated with Faversham. The Faversham hoy, still very obviously related to its Dutch counterpart, was 'sturdy enough to weather the oft-times foul weathers of Sea Reach; shallow enough to creep above Queenhithe and fast enough to make regular passages'.[6] By the early seventeenth century there were eight Faversham corn hoys employed on the London route. Initially built to load twenty to thirty tons apiece, by the eighteenth century they had developed sufficiently to load double that amount into their decked-in holds, where protective hatchboards kept the cargo dry and a small cabin forward was provided for the crew. So seaworthy were the hoys, and such was their ability to sail in any weather, that by the 1720s they were able to provide a reliable timetabled service for both passengers and freight between the Kent ports and London's Bear Key.

As one might expect, it was the various corn crops that provided hoymen with the bulk of their work. These they transported to London throughout the year, but now when to load and sail was governed by the state of the market, rather than the immediate needs of the people to be fed. Dennis Baker explains how the small family businesses which owned the hoys also had close ties with farming in the region, advertising their services in the various inns in Canterbury where they were most likely to attract local custom. The hoymen began to provide further services – organising freights and handling business for their farming customers. In Canterbury and Whitstable large warehouses stood beside the inns where grain and other goods bound for London could be stored. Canny farmers kept a close eye on the Bear Key grain prices which were regularly published in the *Kentish Post*. Once they deemed the price to be right they would issue instructions for their produce to be moved out of store and onto the hoy without delay. This was arranged by the hoyman. Soon he was offering to act as a financial intermediary; in other words by accepting receipts and making payments on behalf of his customers in Kent he effectively took on the role of banker at a time when banking facilities were primitive and unable to cope with the numerous business transactions generated by the middlemen and their markets.[7]

Although there was keen competition between the hoy owners, there was also a high degree of shared interest and dependance between the hoy operators themselves and the farmers with whom many shared bonds of family. So closely knit were they that when threatened by outsiders they were in a position to quickly organise themselves. An incident which occurred in 1732 serves as an example. The buyers of products at Bear Key were responsible for paying the various market dues. Corn unloaded at the quay was bought by a whole range of dealers, both wholesale and retail, and on this occasion they decided to shift the charges onto the sellers, namely the Kent farmers and hoymen. The sellers would have none of it and resolved to petition the Lord Mayor and Common Council of the City of London. They sought and received backing from their counterparts in other districts, with particularly prompt and unequivocal support coming from Faversham. Here, just five years earlier the very first Farmer's Club in the country had been formed by yeoman farmers in the area. It could co-ordinate local opinion and rapidly pass information between its members, many of whom were also hoy owners. Further support quickly came from the men of Milton and Sittingbourne; suffice to say that no more was heard of this 'warm dispute'.[8]

The hoymen were rapidly moving from the role of simple conveyers of goods to that of corn factors. No longer just the paid carriers but also the receivers of consignments at Canterbury or one of the local ports, they transported the grain to Bear Key and once there arranged the unloading by corn meters from boat to quayside and finally its sale to the highest bidder. Baker's research suggests that the freight charges for wheat normally amounted to 5 or 6 percent of the selling price. The farmer paid about 1½d per ton-mile which included the carriage, handling and selling of the crop. Contrast this with the cost by road: in wagons, under the most favourable of conditions, it cost about 7½d. It seems that the cost of transporting goods by water was a fifth of land-carriage costs. Thus hoymen and farmers were greatly dependent upon each other and not simply on the one suppling the product and the other getting it to market, but because between them they could keep the selling price as competitive as possible.

As the amount of business grew it became more usual to bring samples to the market rather than whole loads of corn. Transactions could be conducted rather more rapidly and the deliveries made at a later date. This way of working changed the face of the market, and in 1728 Daniel Defoe noted: 'Instead of the vast number of horses and wagons of corn on market days there were crowds of farmers, with their samples, and buyers such as mealmen, millers, corn-buyers, brewers etc., thronging the market; and on the days between the markets the farmers carried their corn to the hoys and received their pay.'[9] Selling by sample meant it was no longer necessary for factors and dealers to carry on their business outside in all weathers, and in 1750 the Corn Exchange was erected on a newly acquired site in Mark Lane. The day of the corn market regulated by the lord mayor and his burgesses was long since passed. Feeding the people had become a private enterprise with the Kent hoymen playing a significant part in that transformation.

Changes too were rapidly underway in the way that the milling of flour was carried out around London. No longer was the grinding of grain controlled by the Church and the landed gentry. The right of the local lord to demand that the peasantry bring their grain to his mill to be ground, with his bakehouse conveniently situated close by for the baking or purchase of bread from his ovens, was fast disappearing, and no longer was it the job of the miller simply to grind the grain brought to him.

Instead, the owner of either a wind or water mill had become, as Dennis Baker in his essay on the marketing of corn in the eighteenth century, puts it, 'essentially a manufacturer who served the owners by grinding their corn when brought to his mill'.[10] He could buy locally and directly from the grower and fulfill other roles such as that of mealman, flourman and corn merchant. By regular purchases of grain from local sources, a miller could avoid lying idle, waiting to grind what corn was brought to him and ground on commission. After the grinding, he could also seek out the best markets for his flour and his meal. By integrating the several different activities – corn buying, grinding, dealing in meal and flour both wholesale and retail – the miller had much better control over the market and consequently the prices.

Many of the regulations which had controlled the sale of grain and bread for centuries were being swept away, as Daniel Defoe had noticed: 'Millers have cut out the mealmen in the country; and whereas they formerly only ground the corn for the mealmen, they now scorn that trade, buy the corn, and grind it for themselves; so the baker goes to the miller for his meal, and the miller to the market for the corn'. The impact and extent of this is not always easy to determine, however, as Dennis Baker points out:

> We cannot possibly say how much meal and flour was being sent to London from Kentish mills. Those mills on coastal sites, such as Herne, were probably heavily involved in this trade. There is some evidence that London middlemen were investing in mill properties in Kent. Mr Thomas Shelmardine, the owner of a Maidstone waterside mill and granary in 1747, was described as a 'meal-factor and baker in East Smithfield London.' It seems likely that sacks of flour were dispatched from this mill to London regularly through the year. Shelmardine's business activities probably involved, in one way or another, corn-buying, grinding, wholesale and retail dealing in flour and meal, and the baking and retailing to the consumer of the final product. Altogether this would have been a complex and tightly integrated business organization.[11]

Baker goes on to say that the manner in which business was developing in Kent was not peculiar to this county alone but serves to describe, in microcosm, what was taking place all over the country. What was entirely new, though, was the emergence of a separate business class and one no longer controlled or regulated by the City-based guilds in London. This was a more fluid coming together of different interests, able to respond quickly to shifts in market forces. Though crown and aristocracy still owned much of the land, they were no longer wholly in control of the wealth of the country. Much of this now lay in the hands of creative private enterprise and in the manufacture and sale of goods and products. It seems hardly surprising, then, that attention should be turned to finding ways of improving transport systems, so that raw materials could be moved to places of manufacture and the finished merchandise dispatched more efficiently to the marketplace.

Eighteenth Century Bread Recipes

Bread was still an important food source in the eighteenth century. Not only was it a staple, it was an important ingredient in many other foods. It was also a precious commodity and not something to be wasted when a little stale. There are many variations on the bread pudding theme, but the following recipe is particularly good.

THE VERY BEST BREAD PUDDING

This recipe, which Jennifer Stanley adapted from *Primitive Cookery, or the Kitchen Garden Display'd*, published in 1767, is a simple but quite delicious bread pudding to make, and a good way to use up stale bread.

Ingredients:
¾ *cup flour*
1 cup bread crumbs
125 g (4 oz) raisins
2 tablespoons sugar
½ teaspoon ground ginger
2 whole eggs
2 egg yolks
1 cup double cream

Sauce:
⅓ butter
⅓ sugar
⅓ brandy

Preheat oven to 150°C / 350°F / Gas 4. Combine the flour, bread crumbs, raisins, sugar and ginger in one bowl. In another bowl, beat together the eggs, yolks, and heavy cream. Combine all the ingredients to make a nice thick batter. Turn out into a well-buttered dish. Bake for about 45 minutes.

For the sauce: melt butter, add the sugar and brandy. Heat gently to dissolve the sugar and evaporate off the alcohol. Allow the pudding to cool then turn out onto plate, slice and pour the sauce over it.[12]

Panada

Every culture that has bread at its heart has devised ways to use up the smallest scraps of the stalest bread. Panada is probably the most basic and universal of these.

The *Oxford English Dictionary* defines panada as 'A simple dish consisting of bread boiled to a pulp and flavoured.' Gruel, porridge and panada were part of the everyday meals of eighteenth century citizens, from the higher echelons of society to the lowest, and played a key role in the care of infants, the elderly and the sick. Panada was a versatile recipe as it could be made with either savoury or sweet ingredients and eaten as a dish in its own right, but could also be turned into a sweet or savoury sauce, used simply as a thickening agent or for binding various forcemeats together.

Elizabeth Raffald gives recipes for both sweet and savoury panada in her book, *The Experienced English Housekeeper*, published in 1769. Whilst there is no specific reference to the type of bread necessary for panada, William Salmon suggests in his definition that it must include 'pure white bread' and the best quality of wheat. Raffald's recipes demonstrate the variety, creativity and usefulness of this dish, although the more expensive ingredients she suggests, such as Madeira wine and cream, were not readily available to most ordinary people. Their panada would have been closer to a basic gruel of bread, water and a little salt.

SWEET PANADA

Cut all the crust off a penny loaf, slice the rest very thin and put it in a saucepan with a pint of water. Boil it till it is very soft and looks clear, then put in a glass of sack or Madeira wine, grate in a little nutmeg and put in a lump of butter the size of a walnut and sugar to your taste. Beat it exceeding fine then put it in a deep soup dish and serve it up. NB. You may leave out wine and sugar and put in a little good cream and a little salt if you like it better.[13]

SAVOURY PANADA

Grate the crumb of a penny loaf, and boil it in a pint of water, with one onion and a few peppercorns until quite thick and soft, then put in two ounces of butter, a little salt and half a pint of thick cream. Keep stirring it until it is like a thick custard; pour it into a soup plate and serve it up. N.B. You may use sugar and currants instead of onions and pepper-corns if you please.[14]

Chapter Ten

All Systems Go

The importance of river traffic in the eighteenth century cannot be overstated. Thameside towns grew in importance as an increasing amount of country produce was sent to feed the growing population of London.

By the eighteenth century, the river carried copious and regular traffic along the 138-mile stretch from London to Lechlade in Gloucestershire. The opening of the Thames and Severn Canal in 1789 created a continuous waterway from London to the Severn estuary. In 1767, over 56,000 tons of goods passed upstream above Marlow. By 1788-89, the upstream total was over 70,000 tons, with downward traffic almost half as large again. Barge traffic was now a regular feature between Oxford and London and by 1767 many barges had an incredible loading capacity of 200 tons. Sea coal, shipped down the coast and through London, amounting to some 80,000 tons annually was being landed and distributed at the wharves of Reading, Henley, Abingdon and Marlow. Nearly a hundred barges of ever increasing size plied the stretches above London in the later eighteenth century, and some two hundred by the early nineteenth.

With the advent of new canals, trade in both directions was becoming more varied. Freight shipped downriver included iron, copper, tin, manufactured metal goods and bombshells, as well as large numbers of cheeses sent to London from Lechlade. Upstream cargoes included groceries, foreign imports, ashes and rags, and hides bound for Gloucester or Tewkesbury. The Middle Thames continued to supply London with meal, malted barley and increasing amounts of ready-ground flour. Underpinning this expanding traffic and the 'canal mania' of the 1780-1790s were the cost differentials between road and water transport. No matter the improvements in the road network and better built roads, for the bulk movement of heavy goods a well-maintained waterway could offer massive overall savings in the pre-railway age, cutting costs per ton between London to Oxford by over 70 percent in the 1800s.

Both the speed of transport and the safety of goods in transit became hugely important. Many Acts of Parliament at this time centred on attempts to improve transport facilities for the carriage of bulk raw materials and manufactured goods. The death penalty was imposed for stealing from barges and wharves, and for any deliberate destruction of locks and weirs.

In 1751 what would later become the Thames Navigation Commission was set up. It was tasked with overseeing flash locks and the tolls charged for towpaths used by men and horses on the Thames above Staines. However, it met with limited success; its measures annoyed the bargemen with both unrealistic restrictions, and with a temporary adjustment to the tolls charged. In 1770, the Thames Act was enacted. Commissioners, who had noted that parts of the river were becoming impassible at certain times of the year, petitioned Parliament and they were given new powers to acquire land by compulsory purchase, in order to build and improve the locks and weirs.[1]

By 1773, eight pound locks were built between Shiplake Lock and Boulters Lock. The opening of the Thames and Severn Canal in 1789, connecting the two rivers and providing a through route between London and Bristol, led to the building of many of the locks upstream of Shiplake.[2]

Pressure from the Thames and Severn Canal Company and the proprietors of the newly opened Oxford Canal, as well as the plethora of schemes to build various canals which might bypass parts of the Thames, did at least act as a spur to the Commissioners to get on and improve the river under their jurisdiction. Further Acts were passed aimed at reinforcing their existing powers but it was a hugely unwieldy body of minor landowners, town and parish officials, as well as Members of Parliament whose constituencies were in the Thames Valley.

Full of vested interests and often seemingly all pulling in different directions, it took years to carry out the necessary improvements that the Acts demanded. In 1857 the Thames Conservancy, a government appointed body, was formed and in 1866 it became responsible for all river management from Teddington Lock, the last lock on the river, to the head of the navigation. The Thames Conservancy would build more locks over the years; it installed lock keepers, weir keepers and lengthsmen, and it was in charge of setting the amount and collection of tolls. The river had at last become a regulated route for transport purposes rather than an ongoing battleground of vested interests.

By the end of the eighteenth century, in the teeming place that London had become, it was apparent that the old London Bridge – by then over six hundred years old – needed to be replaced. It was narrow and decrepit, slowing the vehicles passing over it to a standstill and blocking the route for through river traffic below. The bridge with its central chapel, some 129 shops and houses up to seven storeys in height, as well as mill and waterwheels, gates and drawbridge must have seemed a most progressive and imposing structure when first built.

The buildings erected upon it paid for its construction and upkeep, along with the tolls charged for its use. Although it was some 8 metres wide, the buildings took up at least 2 metres on either side leaving barely 4 metres for the traffic passing across the bridge. By 1722, congestion was becoming so serious that the Lord Mayor decreed:

All carts, coaches and other carriages coming out of Southwark into this City do keep all along the west side of the said bridge: and all carts and coaches going out of the City do keep along the east side of the said bridge.[3]

New London Bridge showing the busy river.

Thus driving on the left became London's first traffic regulation.

Westminster, London's second bridge, was opened in 1750. Between 1758 and 1762 all the houses and shops on London Bridge were demolished. The two centre arches were replaced by a single wider span in an attempt to improve navigation. These improvements proved to be insufficient and a new London Bridge, situated just 30 metres upstream of the original, constructed with five stone arches across the river, was finally opened in 1831.

The demolition of the old London Bridge and the removal of its massive piers and foundations caused the behaviour of the river to change dramatically. No longer could it impede the ebb and flow of the tide. The sluggish waters above the bridge, which in severely cold winters would freeze to a thickness allowing the famous Frost Fairs to take place, were no more. The river became deeper in places and shallower in others, sand and gravel which had lain peacefully for centuries was scoured out, and the tide flowed fast and unimpeded up to Staines.

With the removal of the bridge, the barges plying their trades on both approaches to London were no longer physically separated by the largely unnavigable bridge. It was probably during this period that both the owners and barge builders from either ends of the river began to take note of the particular features of unfamiliar craft and, where it made sense, incorporate them into the building of subsequent barges of their own. Crude cabins began to appear on the upriver barges, making it easier for the crew to stay on board for days at a time; the swim-ends which helped the 'western' barges to negotiate the flash locks, now fast disappearing, were steadily being replaced with rounder bows and a stem post causing it to 'swim' through the water better and making it easier to tow; the simple flat transom stern became almost universal, as did the large fixed wooden rudder and removable tiller bar. Craft were built with side decks and hatches, so the hold space could be covered in and valuable cargoes protected. The 'stumpy' rig of the hoys and downriver barges, which allowed mast and sails to be dropped quickly and easily with the use of winches, could be adapted for use by craft restricted to more inland waters but with many bridges to negotiate. At last, the whole length of the river, stretching from the Thames estuary to the town of Oxford, could be navigated by barges carrying 100 tons or more.

By the 1790s, other canals were under construction bringing ever greater opportunities for London-based trade and manufacturing industries. The Grand Junction Canal connected London to what were fast becoming the industrial heartlands of the country, in the Midlands and the North. The rivers Lea and Wey, important navigable tributaries of the Thames, were steadily upgraded. Both penetrated into grain growing areas: the Lea into Hertfordshire and the Wey into Surrey, and barges using both contributed to the supply for London of wheat, barley, malt, meal and flour. Great quantities of oats and hay and straw were brought upriver by barge from the farms of Essex, Suffolk and Kent to feed the thousands of horses used for transport in the capital, with backloads of steaming manure collected off the streets and shipped out every day to the surrounding countryside.

In the Port of London, barges threaded their way through the thousands of ships lying at anchor. The City controlled the Empire and here ships laden with valuable cargoes of raw materials from all over the world would wait to be unloaded, and for their cargo of finished goods and manufactured products to be loaded for export. The more prosaic, everyday 'housekeeping' traffic went about its daily round. Cinders and ashes, the byproducts of what was fast becoming a coal-burning city, were valuable ingredients to the burgeoning brick-making industries springing up around London. Regular loads were daily shipped out from the city's vestry wharves via river and canal. Rags, too, for use in papermaking or as manure, and rubbish, all were removed by barge to be dumped in canal-side tips or further down river on the marshes of Essex.

The country was beginning to stir out of its essentially agrarian way of life. There was money to be made out of coal and machinery. The wealthy rushed to capitalize on the country's natural assets and the labour of the peasants, driven off the land to the suburbs of the manufacturing towns, was there to be exploited.

All Systems Go

During the seventeenth and eighteenth centuries, Norfolk, East Anglia, the middle Thames, Sussex and Kent grew enough grain to feed the metropolis and still have a surplus for export. London, however, was not the only city in England experiencing the pressures brought by an industrial and agrarian revolution driving people from the land to the town. They too must be fed. In spite of a huge increase in the amount of land to grow food and the newly developed strains which were producing larger crops of better wheat, the country could not, in the end, continue to be entirely self-sufficient, especially when threatened by a succession of poor harvests. Fortunately each year that there was a bad harvest, the American colonies stepped in to meet the deficit.

For England, still for the most part a net exporter of wheat to the Continent, the emerging American grain trade meant that the two countries were in competition for the same markets. American wheat was of a superior quality and cheaper. It was being grown in great quantities in ideal conditions and harvested by slave labour.

In spite of the long sea passage, the wind driven sailing ships were able to carry several hundred tons at a time, and this kept transport costs low. For London grain traders, America represented both a threat to the marketplace and a promise of salvation when home harvests failed. Throughout the century there were numerous calls by politicians, landowners and farmers to prohibit the export of grain from the colony. Fears were expressed that 'great Quantities of Corn Land' were brought into production and that wheat would be exported into Europe at 'those Places which have always been the British Farmers' Markets'. Parliament was requested to 'prohibit the Exportation of Corn from America into Europe and other Things which may prejudice the British Farmer and Tradesman'. A petition from 'several Merchants of London' in 1749 also makes the point that they are unable to compete with the Americans on exports of wheat to the Continent.[4]

Such demands met with limited success and with the ending of the American War of Independence Britain no longer had the power to exert the same controls and prohibitions it once had over its former colony. Overseas trade was re-opened in 1780. Harvest failures in 1788 and 1789 made Britain's dependence on American imports of wheat all too clear. The years from 1792 are marked by wars and revolutions in Europe, bad harvests both at home and in America, and the ongoing battle with the Hessian fly which decimated crops in the American states. All these events caused huge fluctuations in the price and availability of grain.

With the ending of the Napoleonic Wars the price of wheat fell, and in 1815 the government passed the Corn Laws, which were designed to protect homegrown grain prices against competition from cheaper foreign imports. The ancient Assize of Bread system had become increasingly difficult to enforce in the crowded city and was effectively scrapped, giving bakers the means to determine their own price for a loaf of bread. Undercutting became rife and in an effort to keep the price of a loaf affordable, some bakers resorted to adding potatoes to the bread. Larger milling companies found profit in taking over bakeries and producing bread made from heavily adulterated flour.

When introduced, the Corn Laws of 1815 were aimed at protecting the home farmer and raising revenue. Their effect was to keep the price of English grain artificially high. Their result was to further impoverish an already impoverished working class. The economic issue was that the cost of grain was central to the price of bread, and the working man spent much of his wages on this staple product. The political argument was essentially between landowners who predominated in Parliament and the newer class of manufacturers and industrial workers who, at this point, still had few political representatives. The former wished to maximize their profits from agriculture by keeping the price at which they could sell their grain high. The latter looked to maximize their profits by reducing the wages they paid to their factory workers. However, the difficulty was that men would not work in the factories if a factory wage was not enough to feed them and their families; hence, in practice, high grain prices kept factory wages high also.

Following a series of bad harvests and the catastrophic Irish potato famine, which lasted from 1845 to 1852, successive waves of civil disobedience and rioting occurred across the country and in London; the Corn Laws were eventually repealed in 1846. The price of homegrown cereals began to fall, the amount of land under cultivation declined and Britain became increasingly reliant upon imported grain. Their abolition saw a significant increase in free trade and within a decade American ships were transporting wheat to Britain in ever increasing quantities.

Wheat was not a plant indigenous to America; it was first grown by the English navigator Bartholomew Gosnold, the discoverer of Cape Cod, in 1602 on an island off the Massachusetts coast. The first wheat crops on American soil were sown by immigrant farmers; they planted the golden seed harvested from tiny English fields into the vast, as yet uncharted prairie land that was the New World and then watched it grow. American immigrant farmers were keen to plant new products and utilize new equipment. Unlike their European counterparts they were not mired down by centuries of deep-rooted suspicion of anything new. Rather here 'the new' was grasped by young and enthusiastic men and women who had only the future to look to. While English settlers watched their crops sprout green in the American states, in Canada, a young French chemist, Louis Hébert, who had been granted his land by Louis XIII, was planting wheat in what would one day become the city of Quebec.

In western Canada the settlers were Scotsmen, a small band of sheep herders displaced from their tiny crofts by the Highland Clearances. This group led by their laird, the Earl of Selkirk, settled in the Red River Valley where the river runs from Minnesota into Lake Winnipeg. They arrived unprepared to become crop farmers, yet the wheat they planted flourished and the province of Manitoba became one of the greatest wheat lands in the world. It is true to say that the wheat crops of the New World not only founded a nation but also saved Europe subsequently, over and over again, from starvation.

It was the Gold Rush of 1848 that largely created the impetus for the development of the American export market in grain.

At the time, California's economy was largely agricultural with wheat, along with maize, having been grown as far back as the early eighteenth century by the native American population. It was wheat that was being grown on the farm of a Swiss settler by the name of John Sutter where the first gold was discovered. While his crop was rapidly destroyed by the hordes of miners that descended upon his land, it was wheat that would quickly become the other valuable commodity alongside gold that helped power the Californian economy for the next forty years or more.

Although by the 1840s steam-driven ships were already being built, heralding the eventual demise of the great sailing vessels, then the main carriers of the world's trade, nevertheless it was the American clipper ships, long narrow wooden vessels carrying huge amounts of canvas sail, which were the fastest ocean-going sailing ships in the world that reigned supreme.

Clippers were more dependable than earlier ships. They strained less in heavy seas and crossed belts of calm better than ships carrying less sail. The discovery of gold in California provided another incentive for speed. Clippers carrying their cargoes of gold prospectors and merchandise around Cape Horn to California, would wish to return rapidly for another such cargo. They continued until the end of the century bringing the huge numbers of immigrants from Europe to Californian shores and from there carried away, as return loads, cargoes of wheat which was to become another, rather more sustainable, 'golden' commodity of western America.[5]

The California clippers increased rapidly in size from the 1850s. Grain in 100 lb bags was packed into the holds of ships which were able to load between 1,500 and 2,000 tons register. Wheat production and milling operations grew quickly after the Gold Rush and by 1854 the state was making its first exports to England. From the 1830s to the 1860s, the construction of new railroads flourished across the country.

As the century progressed, networks were constructed in the North and Midwest, and by 1860 all the major cities were linked. In the heavily settled Midwestern Corn Belt, a region of relatively level land and deep, fertile soils high in organic matter, over 80 percent of farms were soon within 5 miles (8 km) of a railway, facilitating the shipment of grain, hogs and cattle to national and international markets. The grain harvest could now be sent in bulk by rail to the East Coast ports, there to be loaded for onward shipment to Europe.

As supplies of grain arrived in London in ever larger volumes from distant places, huge changes in the way that the wheat was supplied induced equivalent changes in marketing methods and the institutions that had traditionally controlled those markets. As the first country to undergo an 'Industrial Revolution' Britain served as the focal point for both buyers and sellers in the nineteenth century grain market. Rather than government intervention which had formerly been the case, with the repeal of the Corn Laws in 1846 it was the diffusion of improved communications and transport that now shaped the market. The mid-nineteenth century press dubbed it 'the revolution of steam and electricity', its shorthand for the distribution of more and better steamboats, railways, telegraph lines and transoceanic cables. These remarkable innovations changed the speed, scale and nature of commercial transactions.

They rapidly made their mark in London. Though homegrown wheat continued to arrive by barge into London, the steady supply of quite small parcels of perhaps up to 200 tons at a time, which could be unloaded and almost immediately sold on to millers and bread suppliers, was now being supplemented by thousands of tons arriving in grain-carrying ships from America and Australia. The ability to store these huge quantities arriving as single bulk cargoes, plus a speedy means to turn them into flour, became crucial.

London, during the eighteenth and nineteenth centuries, had become the busiest port in the world. The Pool of London saw a phenomenal increase in both overseas and coastal trade in the second half of the eighteenth century. Two thirds of coastal vessels using the Pool were colliers meeting an increase in the demand for coal as the population of London rose. Coastal trade virtually doubled between 1750 and 1796, reaching 11,964 vessels in 1795.

As for overseas trade, in 1751 the pool handled 1,682 ships and 234,639 tons of goods. By 1794 this had risen to 3,663 ships and 620,845 tons. By this time the river was lined with nearly continuous walls of wharves running for miles along both banks, with hundreds of ships moored in the river or alongside the quays. It was in this lack of capacity in the Pool of London that London's enclosed docks had their origins.[6]

The building of the Port of London and its modern docks produced a myriad of changes, directly affecting the way grain was conveyed, handled and ultimately turned into the flour needed to keep London fed.

ROBERT MAY'S FRENCH BREAD

Londoners were becoming richer and society more refined. Changing tastes are reflected in more sophisticated recipes like these below, aimed at creating lighter, more digestible breads.

Ingredients:
2 teaspoons active dry yeast
1 teaspoon sugar
1 to 1 ⅓ cups water milk and mixture (preferably in 3:1 ratio)
2 cups all-purpose flour
2 cups wholemeal flour
2 egg whites
1½ to 2 teaspoons salt

Warm a ¼ cup of the water-milk mixture and mix the sugar and yeast into it. Leave for 5 to 10 minutes until it is frothy. Put the egg whites in a small bowl and beat till they are just becoming frothy. Knead the dough by hand or use a machine.

Put the flour mixture, salt, the proofed yeast mixture, the beaten egg whites and the water-milk mixture in the processor bowl and knead like regular bread until you have a soft, smooth and elastic dough.

Add as much flour or water or milk to get this consistency. Shape the dough into a ball and transfer to a lightly oiled bowl, loosely covered with a damp cloth, and leave to rise till soft, spongy and almost double in volume. This should take about an hour or so.

Divide the dough into two equal portions (save a little dough before shaping if you want to make decorations with it), and shape each one into a round or long loaf. Loosely cover with plastic or a light cloth and leave it to rise for about 30 to 45 minutes. Decorate with the spare bit of dough or by slashing the top.

Brush the top of the dough with a little milk and bake at 230°C / 450°F / Gas 8 for 15 minutes. Then turn down the oven temperature to 180°C / 350°F / Gas 4 and bake for a further 15 to 20 minutes until the loaf is brown and sounds hollow when tapped. Let the bread cool completely before slicing.

A MILK LOAF

Ingredients:
4 cups flour
1 teaspoon salt
½ teaspoon sugar
1 packet dry yeast
1 cup milk
1 egg

Warm the milk until tepid, add the sugar and yeast and leave until the mixture is frothy. Sift flour with salt into a bowl and add yeast liquid. Mix to a softish dough, then knead until smooth and satiny. Put the dough into a greased bowl, cover with a light damp cloth, and leave in a warm place to rise until about double in size. Punch down, knead again until smooth and place in a greased loaf tin, 9 x 5 inches.

If you want you can divide the dough into three or four equal pieces after punching down, then with your hands roll each piece into a sausage shape. Place on a baking tray and plait the rolled pieces of dough together, pressing the ends together firmly to make them secure. Brush the plait with a glaze of beaten egg yolk mixed with a couple of tablespoons of milk. Sprinkle with poppy seeds. Leave to prove again.

Bake in a preheated oven 220°C / 425°F / Gas 7 for about 40 minutes. Check it is done by tapping the underside for a hollow sound. Cool on a wire rack.

Chapter Eleven

Everything's Happening

The eighteenth and nineteenth centuries were indeed revolutionary in the sense that they turned most aspects of domestic and industrial life on their heads. The speed of change too was phenomenal, driven largely by those looking for wealth and profit. People continued to flee the countryside for the cities and while many came filled with energy and new ideas, ready to invest them in the developing technology, even more arrived looking for no more than the most basic of livings in the new industrial centres of the country. The daily wage for a working man in the nineteenth century was little changed in terms of what it could buy from that of his earlier fourteenth century counterpart. The purchase of bread and ale still accounted for a large part of his earnings. Feeding the thousands remained the most basic requirement.

As the eighteenth century progressed, coal-fired steam power spread its potential in every direction. The invention of the steam engine opened the way for coal-fired machinery to take over from those centuries-old suppliers of natural energy, wind and water. In 1786, London's first steam-driven mill, Albion Mills, was erected on the banks of the Thames. The Albion flour mill opened at the southern end of Blackfriars Bridge in London and was one of the most visible symbols of Britain's rapid industrial progress. The building contained revolutionary steam engines engineered to the designs of James Watt and Matthew Boulton. Barges delivered the grain directly into the basement of the unimposing building.

Inside the mill, two 50-horsepower steam engines together operated twenty pairs of millstones. The sheer power of the engines promised staggering levels of output in the milling of corn for flour, at a time when London's rapidly growing population was creating a seemingly endless demand for bread. As such, Albion Mills was widely resented by existing millers in London, who were still reliant on water or wind power and who saw the arrival of steam as a death sentence for their businesses.

On 2 March 1791, just five years later, Albion Mills was totally destroyed by fire, an event that caused much rejoicing in some quarters. For others, the whole episode stood as a metaphor for the potential harm caused by industrial progress. Most famously it is thought that the poet William Blake, who lived nearby, was inspired by the burnt shell of the building to portray his vision of 'dark satanic mills', in which the pastoral godliness of England is forever shattered by the infernal fires of industry.[1] Nevertheless, Albion Mills was indeed a foretaste of what was to come: the industrialization of flour. Its erection is the marker for the progression by which the making of bread in London would cease to be a wholly artisanal production, where the flour was milled in relatively small quantities, and the dough was largely mixed by hand and baked in local bakeries by and for those who lived and worked in the immediate neighbourhood.

London's port had become the entrepôt of England. Records show that by 1792 London dealt with 65 percent of all imports. The place was heaving, the river hugely congested; at its busiest, the Upper Pool accommodated 1,775 vessels, all awaiting the services of wharfingers, meter men and lighterage. Part of the problem lay with shipping technology, which lagged far behind the needs of a booming economy: the ships were too small, their hold capacity too limited.

Loading and unloading, the conveying of cargo from ships at anchor to the quayside, required the services of thousands of lighters, adding further to the congestion and making it impossible for the craft crowding the waterway to move up and down the river easily. Lighters loaded with goods were left at anchor, unattended, for weeks as overcrowded wharves and warehouses sought to deal with the massive flow of imports and exports. Not surprisingly they were easy pickings for thieves, with whole bargeloads of goods being emptied in the darkness of night. The business of the river was getting out of hand and required attention; something had to be done. The Port of London Authority's own history underlines the situation:

> The wharf proprietors resisted every effort to provide the addition of a single foot of accommodation. So crowded and over burdened did the Port become that trade and navigation were carried on under difficulties which must soon have diverted a large measure of its commerce to other ports. Eventually in 1796 a Parliamentary Committee of the House of Commons was 'appointed to enquire into the best mode of providing sufficient accommodation for the increased trade and shipping of the Port'.
>
> The Committee prepared an exhaustive report but did not succeed in formulating any definite recommendations for improving matters. Despite the urgency of the situation, it was not until 1799 that Parliament authorised the construction of a dock on the Isle of Dogs 'for rendering more commodious and better regulating the Port of London' and in particular to secure that 'West India produce might be effectually secure from loss by theft or other causes and the public revenue greatly benefited'.[2]

This heralded the building of the first enclosed London dock. Following this, during the nineteenth century, a number of enclosed dock systems were built, each surrounded by high walls to protect cargoes from river piracy. These included West India Dock (1802), East India Dock (1803), London Docks (1805), the Surrey Commercial Dock (1807), St. Katherine's Dock (1828), Royal Victoria Dock (1855), Millwall Dock (1868), Royal Albert Dock 1880), and Tilbury Docks (1886). Built by a number of private companies, the creation of this intricate network of impounded water was a vast industrial undertaking and involved thousands of people, including engineers, architects and surveyors, as well as and huge numbers of labourers.

In order to secure the land for their building, the proprietors had to apply to Parliament. The acts which created the enclosed docks were private acts, so named because they gave powers or benefits to particular individuals or bodies rather than to the general public as a whole. Parliament's role was to arbitrate between the promoters of these private acts and those affected by their projects, as well as to take account of the public interest.

The lightermen fought proposals for the new enclosed docks and petitioned Parliament. They saw their livelihoods disappearing, because ships using the docks would be able to load and unload their cargo directly onto the quayside, store their goods in the new warehouses, and complete their onward journey by road. Although construction went ahead anyway, the lightermen's concerns were recognized, and as a result the West India Dock Act of 1799 – and all subsequent acts relating to the docks – contained a major concession. The 'free water clause' stated that no charges were to be made for 'lighters or craft entering into the docks…to convey, deliver, discharge or receive ballast or goods to or from on board any ship…or vessel.'[3] Its intention was to ensure that lightermen had the same freedom to operate their craft in the new docks as they had on the river. This apparently simple ruling proved costly for the dock owners, allowing wharf owners and lighterage companies to send craft into the docks to load and unload ships directly into lighters, bypassing quay dues and dock warehouses. This small exemption effectively boosted the profits of the dock owners' riverside competitors and had a significant influence on the Port of London's affairs.[4]

The construction of the enclosed docks meant hard times for the riverside wharves. Each new dock company received a 21-year monopoly on handling the goods in which it specialized. This took much valuable commerce away from the traditional wharves lining the river, as the traffic would now be handled instead in the new docks. Although the wharfingers received compensation for their

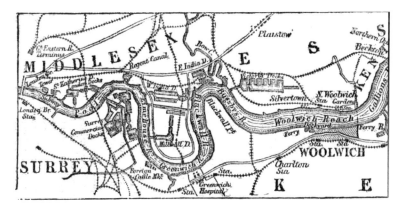

Early map of the enclosed docks.

lost trade, they were forced to concentrate on goods the docks would not handle. At the end of the monopoly period, those wharf-owners who had survived were again able to compete for the many types of business formerly lost.

Further competition became possible with the passing of the Customs Consolidation Act in 1853, which allowed many wharves to handle dutiable goods on the same basis as the docks. The principle of bonded warehouses had been introduced in 1803 and for years the privilege was restricted to the warehouses of the dock companies, which meant that many shipping companies had no choice but to use the docks. Later legislation coincided, more or less, with the termination of the 21-year monopoly period granted to the dock companies, and extended the bonding facilities to the riverside wharf and warehouse proprietors. Although theoretically the shipowners now had a greater freedom of choice between the river wharves or using the docks, with ships getting bigger all the time the spacious new docks were still preferable to the cramped conditions of most of the wharves.

Crucially, the wharves were able to take full advantage of the free water clause; a practice which proved highly damaging to the dock owners. Ships coming into the docks could be loaded and unloaded overside, with barges and lighters transferring their cargoes to and from the riverside wharves rather than to the dock quays, thus bypassing dues for landing and warehousing.

It significantly reduced the docks' income and harmed their finances. Not surprisingly, the dock owners lobbied vigorously, but unsuccessfully, for the abolition of this damaging advantage.

The dock companies began to feel the full effect of the privileges accorded to the lightermen by Parliament. By 1887, the London and St. Katharine Docks Company, which also owned the Royal Victoria and Royal Albert Docks, and the East and West India Docks Company, which had built the Tilbury Dock, were in a bad financial position and were driven to look for some mutually agreeable working arrangement. Whilst the apparent inequity of the 'free water clause' was hugely damaging to the dock owners, it was a lifeline for the lighterage industry, the wharf owners and for river transport as a whole. Without it, in all likelihood most goods during the years of monopoly in particular, would have been landed where the ships docked, with the subsequent demise of much of the water-based transport on the Thames.

An unlooked for consequence of the 'free water clause' was the power it gave to lightermen to control the movement of labour within the Port of London. The Company of Watermen and Lightermen had monopolized river work for centuries and all lightermen were licensed men. The clause forced great changes to the river trade during the period of the Industrial Revolution and later. Dock workers and lightermen fought hard to improve their conditions and were amongst the most militant of labour groups. With unionization and later with the creation of the National Dock Labour Scheme in 1947, they strengthened their grip on the Port of London and its river. The port provided London with its great wealth and it relied heavily on the transhipping skills of the dockers and lightermen to run smoothly. The freights, offloaded from ships to barges and lighters, could be moved out to continue their journeys along what had by now become an integrated river and canal system giving access to the Midlands, to the east coast and inland to the west of England. This was to be a boom time for lighterage, canal transport and barge traffic.

Barges and lighters loading and moving grain thrived, and in spite of the rapid development of better roads and railways directly

Lighters being poled out of Regent's Canal Dock.

Early methods of mechanical loading in St. Katherine's Dock.

connected to the docks, it was those two somewhat anomalous pieces of legislation – the earlier 'eastabout-westabout charter' (said to have been granted to grain carrying bargemen and exempting them from having to use registered lightermen on their craft) and the 'free water clause' (which gave them entry to the docks without charge) – that underpinned the principle of unrestricted movement of grain on the river and probably enabled it to continue for at least another hundred years.

Granaries and mills had always been a distinctive feature of London's waterfront. Most were found in Bermondsey and Rotherhithe. From 1864, with overseas grain ships arriving with loads of a thousand tons or more, granaries were being built with integrated silos for bulk storage. Some granaries also operated mills and these were to be found on some of the largest riverside frontages. Many of the riverside warehouses associated with the granaries were operated by seed and rice merchants, which meant that granary owners could manage an array of dry foodstuffs that needed specialist handling, storage, sampling and preparation for the market. Where there was a mill on the site as well, it meant that these various foodstuffs could be ground, 'flaked' and cleaned. Increasingly sophisticated means of processing and packaging goods were stimulated by the trade, and in Mark Lane in the City of London agents sold grain-handling, processing and milling equipment. After 1880, some warehouses introduced elevators for the discharge of bulk grain. Bagged cereals continued to be discharged by simple overhead hoists.

Any number of other events contributed to the way grain was handled and carried on London's waterways. No longer was it just English grain being brought in river barges to supply the London millers or to be sent on for export. Instead, each year ships which were becoming ever larger, loaded with imported grain, were arriving from the Baltic, Australia, Canada and the Americas. The space provided by the off-river docks meant that huge waterside grain stores could be erected. Ships could discharge directly into them. New machinery operated by hydraulic power systems made it easier and quicker to unload. First used to power coal derricks at Poplar Dock and Regent's Canal Dock, by 1857 all of the older docks on the north side of the river had hydraulic power systems; the newer docks had them from their inception. Soon numerous wharves were also installing their own hydraulic power. With many ships now arriving with holds full of loose wheat, steam-powered cranes could bucket the grain out of the moored ships and load it directly into the waiting lighters and barges. They in turn could transport it out of London to supply mills much further afield. Domestically, grain was still the most important freight, along with coal, to be carried on the river but now its journey was reversed. It flowed from London out to the towns and the countryside. Flour, too, now milled in the docks could be loaded and taken to other destinations by barge.

The ill-fated Albion Mills had been far ahead of its time; for most of the nineteenth century the majority of flour mills in England remained small. On the outskirts of London, a number of windmills continued in business much as they always had. Several smaller steam mills were located on the Thames and its tributaries. For example on the River Lea at Bromley, the Sun Flour Mills received grain from lighters and small craft, and at Deptford Creek, Mumford's Flour Mills, founded in 1790, were supplied by small barges entering the creek from the Thames. Mumford's Mills flourished throughout the nineteenth century and were rebuilt in 1897.

In time though, the smaller mills were to be eclipsed by larger concerns such as Rank, Spillers and the Co-operative Wholesale Society, which set up huge mills receiving imported grain directly through the Royal Victoria Dock. In the twentieth century, this dock became the leading centre of flour milling in London. Three large mills were built on the south side, and here imported wheat was turned into flour for the London market.

With its seven famous windmills along the Mill Wall, the Isle of Dogs had been an important site in medieval times for the grinding of grain. Flour milling returned to the area with the opening of the Millwall Docks in 1868. These docks had been built especially to handle grain imports and offered better facilities for unloading

Flour mill and lock with barges unloading.

grain than any of the other docks in London. Though it failed to capture the grain coming from North America, Millwall Docks instead specialized in imports from the Baltic, brought mostly in Scandinavian sailing ships.

The first large mill to be built alongside any of the London docks was the Wheatsheaf Mill, which stood on the southern quay of the Millwall Outer Dock. Its construction was started in 1869 by the Manchester-based McDougall Brothers, who had pioneered self-raising flour five years earlier. The firm of McDougall Brothers was the first of Britain's giant flour milling concerns. The Wheatsheaf Mill, rebuilt several times over the following century, became one of the major landmarks of the Isle of Dogs. In 1903 the Central Granary was opened at the Millwall Dock. This used Britain's first pneumatic suction elevator, patented by Frederick Duckham, the Millwall Dock Company's resident engineer, and it revolutionized the handling of grain, which was sucked out instead of being scooped up by buckets as before, greatly speeding up the unloading of grain ships. The granary was capable of storing 24,000 tons of grain, and was equipped with appliances that could handle 500 tons of grain per hour.

With Britain now a country no longer reliant upon its own grain crop to feed itself and imported grain becoming the norm, it ultimately led to changes in every element that culminated in the production of a loaf of bread. By the late nineteenth century, some 90 percent of wheat was imported. After the repeal of the Corn Laws in 1846 and then particularly after 1870, Britain began importing vast quantities of wheat from North America, Russia and eastern Europe, India, Australia, and Argentina. The numbers are astounding: in 1850, Britons grew about three-quarters of what they ate. By 1900, they grew less than one-fifth.

Virtually all of this imported wheat was of a 'harder' variety, in that it contained more gluten and was naturally higher in protein than native soft wheats. This resulted in well-risen, lighter loaves of white bread. At the same time, however, it was found that the harder wheat varieties did not grind so well on stones as the native crop; the bran shatters and discolours the flour. Hard wheat needed to be ground with iron rollers. These were first introduced in Britain in the 1870s. Known as roller milling, it is a totally different process to stone milling. Using stones, every part of the grain is pulverized. With rollers, there is a much more gradual process of reduction, where the wheat is 'broken' to remove the bran, then sifted into different sized particles, 'broken' again, sifted again, and so on. This allows the miller to obtain a much whiter flour and much more of it, and allows for greater precision in the grading of flour. One further advantage is that this method of milling leaves less oil in the flour with the result that the baked loaf lasts longer. It was only when virtually all milling was done with rollers that widespread consumption of the unadulterated white bread which graces the shelves of our supermarkets today became the norm.

It was the rapid increase in imported wheat which stimulated the development of roller milling. From the early 1880s, as the national demand for white well-risen loaves became overwhelming, roller milling rapidly replaced millstones and fine white flour produced on an industrial scale started to take over. Many traditional rural mills were no longer able to compete, especially as new railway systems could bring the finished manufactured product right into the heart of their markets. Although water mills were still being used during this period, they were rapidly replaced, particularly in and around London, by the new steam-driven mills. Coal was cheap and available. Mills now no longer needed to depend upon the vicissitudes of wind and water and despite initial problems with steam engines, they soon became more efficient. Nonetheless where water and windmills still ground local grain for their local communities, they were able to carry on much as before, with their more bucolic customers continuing to prefer the darker, heavier, stoneground bread they were used to. In the end though, by the start of the twentieth century, almost all rural mills had ceased commercial production.

In London, Waterloo Bridge Mills and St. Saviour's Mill, both stone grinding mills with thirty and twenty pairs of stones respectively, the latter working on a combined stone and roller system, were converted to full roller milling in 1884-85. Both new mills were capable of producing 45 sacks an hour. Meanwhile 11 of the 20 pairs of stones at Westminster Bridge Mills were replaced by a new roller plant with a capacity of 11 sacks per hour, powered by a 50-horsepower beam engine.

Further away from London, many mills, especially those conveniently situated beside canals and rivers, changed from stoneground to roller milling and continued to receive their wheat supplies in the traditional way – conveyed in barges and brought by water. The essential difference now was that this grain was imported hard wheat and came from the London docks.

Nineteenth Century Bread Recipes

The range of products using wheat flour – breads, cakes and pastries – expanded rapidly from the eighteenth century onwards. The establishment of an educated urban middle class able to buy fine white flour, employ cooks to make and bake all sorts of sweet fancies and desserts in the new-fangled ovens installed in their own kitchens with cookery books to hand, created a market for baking utensils, tinware, and timesaving devices.

Hot Buttered Toast and English Muffins

Although making toast can hardly be called a recipe, it is nevertheless interesting to see the precision of description that young wives were deemed to need in what we might consider the most obvious of tasks, such as in this recipe from Isabella Beeton's celebrated *Book of Household Management*, published in the mid-nineteenth century. As Bill Bryson put it, Beeton's book was 'an instruction manual that could be followed religiously and that was exactly what people wanted'.[5]

TO MAKE HOT BUTTERED TOAST

A loaf of household bread about two days old answers for making toast better than cottage loaf, the latter not being a good shape, and too crusty for the purpose. Cut as many nice even slices as may be required, rather more than ¼ inch in thickness, and toast them before a very bright fire, without allowing the bread to blacken, which spoils the appearance and flavour of all toast. When of a nice colour on both sides, put it on a hot plate; divide some good butter into small pieces, place them on the toast, set this before the fire and when the butter is just beginning to melt, spread it lightly over the toast. Trim off the crust and ragged edges, divide each round into 4 pieces, and send the toast quickly to table. Some persons cut the slices of toast across from corner to corner, so making the pieces of a three-cornered shape. Soyer [Alexis Soyer, the French celebrity chef of the time] recommends that each slice should be cut into pieces as soon as it is buttered, and when all are ready, that they should be piled lightly on the dish they are intended to be served on. He says that by cutting through four or five slices at a time, all the butter is squeezed out of the upper ones, while the bottom one is swimming in fat liquid. It is highly essential to use good butter for making this dish.[6]

MUFFINS

Have you seen the muffin man?
The muffin man, the muffin man.
Have you seen the muffin man
Who lives down Drury Lane?

These were popular during the nineteenth century when men with trays of warm muffins walked the streets at teatime, ringing their bells and selling their wares. In the 1840s the muffin man's bell was prohibited by an Act of Parliament because people objected to the noise, though the ban proved largely ineffective. This is Paul Hollywood's recipe for the classic English muffin:

Ingredients:
300 g (10 ½ oz) strong white bread flour, plus extra for flouring
6 g (¼ oz) fast action yeast
6 g (¼ oz) salt

15 g (½ oz) caster sugar
15 g (½ oz) softened butter, cut into small pieces
1 medium free-range egg, lightly beaten
170 ml (6 fl oz) milk (should make a soft dough – you can add up
to about 30 ml (1 fl oz) extra if needed)
oil, for greasing
15 g (½ oz) semolina or polenta, plus extra for dusting

Tip the flour into a large mixing bowl. Sprinkle the yeast on one side of the flour and the salt into the other side of the flour. Add the sugar, butter, egg and milk, then mix all the ingredients together to form a soft dough. Turn the mixture out of the bowl onto a lightly floured surface and knead for 10 minutes, or until soft, smooth and stretchy. Lightly grease a large bowl with oil. Place the dough in the oiled bowl, cover and leave to prove for about one hour, or until doubled in size.

Dust the work surface with a mixture of the semolina/polenta and flour. Tip the dough out onto the work surface and roll out to about 2.5 cm thick.

Lightly dust two baking trays with half of the semolina or polenta. Using a 9 cm (3 ½ in) straight-sided cutter, cut out eight muffins. Place four muffins, evenly spaced apart on each of the dusted baking trays. Dust the remaining semolina or polenta over the top of the muffins. Leave to prove for another 30 minutes.

Preheat the hot plate or a heavy-based frying pan on the hob to a very low heat. Griddle the muffins for approximately 5 to 6 minutes, then flip over and griddle for another 5 to 6 minutes on the other side. Slice open while still warm, slather with butter, and enjoy.[7]

Chapter Twelve

Steam, Tugs and Sailing Barges

With the building of the enclosed docks came the need to regulate the river. Now that congestion from moored craft in the tideway itself had eased, a new factor, steam power, was destined to change river life yet again.

The new paddlewheel-driven steamers were faster, more versatile and more efficient than the sail and row boats traditionally used to convey people along the Thames and its estuary. At least eighty steamers were recorded operating along the river between the advent of the first steam tug in 1816 and the rise of the railways in southern England in the 1840s. Concerns were voiced early on about the dangers this represented, and the Steamboat Act of 1819 was the first piece of legislation to address public safety in relation to this new form of travel.[1]

As more steam tugs arrived on the river their superior power and manoueverability in towing and docking the sailing ships that brought freight and passengers to London became obvious. Initially, watermen and lightermen were hostile to this new technology, seeing it as a threat to their livelihoods. However, they were forced to recognize the ascendency of this new way of working on the river and so turned their attention instead to ensuring that the operation of tugs and passenger boats became part of their remit.

Though the days of the great ocean-going sailing ships were clearly numbered, it was not until 1875 that sail took second place in the tonnage using the port; in that year steam represented 5.1

million tons and sail only 3.6 million.[2] Even so, the use of tugs in the river was not restricted to the manoeuvering of sailing ships. Steam ships too, by virtue of their greater size, needed the assistance of tugs to escort them up and down the river, into the docks and onto their berths. In spite of the advance of steam power, it was sail that continued to deliver the cargoes of grain, tea and sugar from across the world and the forest-like appearance of the port, characterized by the tall masts and rigging of hundreds of sailing ships, was still much in evidence well into the twentieth century.

The opening of the Suez canal gave great impetus to the changeover from sail to steam. When it opened in 1869 it provided a shortcut for steamships to Asia. However, they were burdened by their dependence on coal. As the distance a steamship travelled increased, so did the amount of cargo space required to hold the coal and the further it travelled, all else being equal, the more it cost. When sailing ships were displaced, it was first on short distance routes, then, as steamship technology improved, on progressively longer distance routes. This diffusion of steamships depended on cargo technology, currents and infrastructure. In many countries of the world neither coal as a commodity, nor the newer techniques in shipbuilding, were so freely available as in Britain. Often ports could not accept these new large vessels or had not installed the modern equipment needed to handle their cargoes. In any case, sailing ships were large capital investments, not to be cast away until their useful life was over, especially as their source of motive power was free. Though steam power promised to free ocean vessels from the whims of wind and weather, in its early days they suffered from a variety of problems: carrying enough fuel, finding reliable engines, and supporting huge operating costs.

Nevertheless, steam inexorably began to replace sail, and by the second half of the nineteenth century it was widely being used for ocean commerce. The earliest vessels were hybrids that relied on both steam engines and sails, like the American-built *Savannah* which made the first steam-assisted crossing of the Atlantic in 1819. Regular steamship crossings didn't begin until the 1840s, but by

Pool of London showing steam and sail.

the 1850s many wealthier passengers took steamships, though most immigrants still crossed the ocean under sail. The great clippers continued to crowd the London docks right up until the eve of World War II. Grain ships like the *Moshulu*, winner of the last grain race from Australia to Britain, loaded with 59,000 sacks of grain, some 4,785 tons in all, could still give steam power a run for its money. For the movement of worldwide cargoes, steam ships only finally replaced sail once they became larger and faster and could be shown to be more regular and reliable.

The development of the oceangoing steamship was preceded by smaller vessels used for internal transportation. When the technology of steam was mastered at this level, steam engines were installed on larger craft and, eventually, on oceangoing vessels. Once it was proved, and the vessels were propelled by screw rather than paddle wheels, the new technology caused the very design of ships' hulls to change so as to achieve faster, more economic propulsion.

Steam tugs rapidly replaced all earlier forms of manpowered towage in the Port of London. No longer was it sensible or even necessary for gangs of men in rowing boats to drag sailing ships up and down the river. It was not long, however, before the tugs, which required fewer men and had a speedier turnround, found themselves part of the unceasing competition between the dock companies. Vessels could be towed more cheaply and easily to upriver docks, bypassing and undercutting those situated further downstream. In time, propellor-driven tugs would supercede the paddlers, though paddle-driven steam tugs continued to be built throughout the nineteenth century, only finally being phased out in the 1920s by diesel power.[2]

Though the lightermen initially fought against their introduction to the river, it was not long before the advantages of using tugs to tow lighters became blindingly obvious. Towing by tug speeded up the whole operation of moving craft of all sizes around, both on the river and in the enclosed docks. One knock-on effect was that ships could be built even larger once it became established practice to use tugs to manoeuvre them in confined areas. With the development of steam tugs the bigger sailing ships, normally too large to negotiate the enclosed docks on their own, could now be brought in off the river with the help of one or two tugs, and berthed directly on the dockside.

The river itself, already hemmed in for miles with wharves, warehouses and factories, was to be further contained. The embankment on the northern side of the river, designed by Sir Joseph Bazalgette, was begun in 1862. Bazalgette's embankment narrowed the river as he reclaimed and utilized some 22 acres (89,000 square metres) of river bank. The foreshore where barges and lighters had once moored was swallowed up. Instead, beneath the new road and walkway, he was able to accommodate the main west London sewer and an underground railway.[3]

Now with a mix of craft – sail, steam and oars – navigating in the increasingly narrow confines of the Thames and with a swifter current to contend with, rammings and sinkings of unpowered craft by these new fast moving steam-driven vessels became a frequent occurrence. The rule that steam must give way to sail and rowed craft only served to increase the discord. Watermen and lightermen complained of the turbulence caused by steamers, and the masters of steamers cursed the lumbering barges that got in their way.

An administrative change to how the river was run was becoming essential. Most of the grievances expressed by the merchants – the owners of the goods passing through the Port of London – of inadequate space on the water, on the riverside, and in the warehouses, had been met by building the enclosed docks. Now it was the turn of shipowners to complain about the lack of depth of water for their craft, and the need to regulate navigation. With the advent of steam power a state of chaos existed, with tugs and passenger boats racing along, disrupting slower traffic, undermining river banks, and causing damage to property, not to mention considerable loss of life.

Finally, in 1857, after years of lobbying, the Thames Conservancy Act was passed. This gave the Conservators 'all title and rights in the bed and foreshore of the river from Staines to Yantlet Creek and empowered them to carry out all conservancy duties, including the proper regulation of river traffic and the maintenance of the navigation channel'.[4]

There can be no doubt that by the end of the nineteenth century the desired increase in ship size had come about, but with it came a concomitant increase in draught. Larger vessels required deeper channels in the river and in the docks. What needed to be done was obvious, but the power to implement changes was bogged down by the various companies and authorities involved. The problems were exacerbated by the dock companies, who were in a bad way financially, as competition between themselves and the river wharves had taken its toll.

For the dock companies the 'free water clause' had done irreparable damage, depriving them of revenue from locking and landing charges, and warehouse rental. In the hopes of ameliorating its position, the London and India Docks Joint Committee deposited a bill in Parliament in 1899, which sought to give them powers to charge barges and lighters entering their docks and to extract a toll for all the goods moved by these craft. This did not go down well, according to the Port of London Authority:

> The Bill aroused great opposition and was rejected. The Government were, however, impressed with the seriousness of affairs and announced that as the Port of London presented a problem of such importance from a national point of view a Royal Commission would be appointed to inquire fully into the matter. The Commission sat for two years and in June 1902 issued a comprehensive report containing recommendations for the creation of a central authority.[5]

Even so, it was not until 1908 that a measure was passed to become law under the title of the Port of London Act, 1908. It transferred the undertakings and powers of all the existing companies in the enclosed docks, as well as the function and powers of the Thames Conservancy below Teddington, and certain duties of the Watermen's Company, to a new body: the Port of London Authority (PLA).

Steam, Tugs and Sailing Barges

The PLA's primary duty was, in the words of the Act of 1908, 'to take into consideration the state of the river and the accommodation and facilities afforded in the Port of London, and, subject to the provisions of this Act, to take such steps as they may consider necessary for the improvement thereof'.[6] Broadly speaking, the Act gave it control of all matters relating to ships and shipping, both in the docks and on the main river. Though the wharves remained in private hands, ownership of the enclosed docks passed to the PLA. Powers such as the registration and licensing of craft, lightermen and watermen, which had hitherto been within the remit of the Watermen's Company, now became part of the PLA's duties.[7]

A large element of competition remained in the Port; the riverside wharves were outside the Authority's jurisdiction, except for certain conservancy matters, and traded independently. The proprietors of the private wharves and warehouses continued to enjoy, directly and indirectly, the advantages of the free use of the docks by barges under the 'free water clause'.

The Port of London, under the jurisdiction of the PLA, now stretched from immediately below Teddington Lock all the way downstream to Yantlet Creek, which separates the Isle of Grain from the Hoo Peninsula in Kent.

In spite of huge strides in modernizing both the Port and the river itself, the way that grain came into London and was despatched from there both in its raw state or as refined flour changed very little. The battle to survive against more modern forms of transport was ongoing and though this battle would be slowly lost, it was the ability of small craft – lighters, barges and canal boats – to load directly off ships and from bankside silos that allowed an increasingly archaic form of transport to survive for as long as it did.

Where once barges arrived in London from both upstream and down with loads of homegrown grain, now they came to load the cheaper foreign wheat being imported into London's docks. Taken directly overside from the ship, it could be sent downriver to millers on the rivers Stour and Orwell west of the Thames, up the rivers Lea, Stort and Wey, and far inland by canal to the very centre of England.

To move grain and other goods up and down the tidal river and estuary a very particular kind of craft was required: one that could handle small cargoes economically, one that was robust enough to come alongside cargo ships and liners in the Pool of London, but which was also able to negotiate the shallow waters of East Anglia.

The Thames barge, which became such a familiar part of the English mercantile scene, had its antecedents in the Netherlands, like the hoy. The hull, so similar to the crude Thames lighter with its box-like hold and swim ends, began to edge towards the rounded bow shape of the Dutch hoys. A more shapely bow set into an upright stempost let it cut cleanly through the water. The flat transom stern, borrowed from seagoing sailing ships, allowed more deck space where a man could stand to steer, room for a cabin below, added buoyancy and a better flow of water around the stern.

Hull improvements made for a craft with better handling and a hold which carried maximum payload, but the glory of the Thames barge was its arrangement of sails. The spritsail rig originated in Holland and was introduced in around 1420. Adopted by smaller hoys, smacks and wherries because of its simplicity and ease of handling, it soon gravitated onto larger working craft.[8] The average size of a Thames barge was between 80 to 90 feet (24-27 metres) with a beam of about 20 feet (6 metres). It loaded about 120 tons of cargo with 4,200 square feet (390 square metres) of canvas between six working sails. The spritsail rig was carried on two masts: the main and the mizzen. The main mast supported a topsail above a huge mainsail and a large foresail. The mizzen carried a single sail whose main purpose was to aid steering when tacking. The spritsail rig was better at turning to windward than almost any other form of sail, and with its large sail area on the upper part of the mast it could catch even the lightest of winds.

For two hundred years Thames barges had moved around the Thames and Medway rivers in a somewhat ponderous way, with very little change in design. Then in the 1860s the barge match – a series of barge races – was introduced, and so intense was the competition that barge design improved significantly, as their owners sought to win these prestigious matches.[9]

The improvements in hull form and rigging were a direct result of the races and allowed this cumbersome vessel to become highly manoeuvrable – crucial when negotiating the busy Pool of London. The better hull shape and sail arrangement turned it from a clumsy riverbound workhorse into an elegant, speedy and economical seagoing vessel, able to withstand virtually any weather to be found in the North Sea and the Thames Estuary.

Flat-bottomed, it could rest on mud, shingle or sand exposed by the receding tide and, just as importantly, it was able to run empty with assistance from leeboards, without the need for ballast. The masts could be speedily lowered without having to furl the sails when passing under bridges and then heaved back up on the other side while the barge was still under way.[10] They were as equally suited to creeping along shallow tidal creeks on the east coast as navigating their way through the congested docks of London.

A Thames spritsail barge had, at most, a crew of three: skipper, mate and boy. Owners provided their keep, but wage packets were small. Extra pay was earned by loading and unloading their craft, which meant manhandling as much as 200 tons in a working day.[11] Handling bricks, coal, grain, rubbish or manure, it was dirty, back-breaking and exhausting work, and done by the same men who knew every set of the tide, every current and sandbank, who could taste the wind and know when to set the sails. With few aids – a compass perhaps, a sextant was rarely used – they relied on their own skill and knowledge learned on the job, handing it down from father to son, master to mate, man to boy.

In the nineteenth century, there were thousands of barges working the Thames; even in the middle of the twentieth century it was still a common sight to see fifty or more lying at anchor in the esturial rivers, waiting for the tide or a fair wind into London.[12] With their tanned sails, bright paintwork and bold scrollwork at bow and stern, these beautiful utilitarian craft have been beloved by both artists and historians for generations and are very well documented.[13]

Upstream, their less elegant cousins, the inland barges, evolved in a somewhat different way to the estuarial barge. Barge building on the non-tidal Thames and its associated waterways was very localized and each developed a slightly different craft adapted for local conditions. Although the basic shape and length to beam ratio was similar, craft could vary widely depending on the waterway and the work to be done. Locks and bridges, in particular, determined the size and shape of a barge: the inward slope of a boat's bulwarks and cabin sides could be quite pronounced to prevent catching on bridges, and straight-sided hulls were essential for passing through locks. All fell within the genre of 'western barges' though one from the River Kennet would be recognizably different to one from the Thames and Severn Canal.

These unpowered craft, either worked by men on board or towed, no longer subject to the damage inflicted by the flash locks and rarely to the rigours of wind, weather and tide, were altogether simpler in design, though strongly built. The primitive hooped canvas awning which had served as crews' quarters was replaced by a more substantial cabin with a bunk or two, and a simple bottle stove for when crew stayed onboard overnight. Sails to augment towing were still used, but by the 1850s the crudely rigged square sail had been replaced by the more responsive spritsail. The more sophisticated design improved the efficiency of the craft and better cabins the lives of those on board. Nevertheless, in spite of their improved design and greater efficiency, for the great bulk of inland craft the introduction of railways was to herald their decline and ultimate doom.

Despite huge opposition from many quarters including the Thames Commissioners and the City of London, Brunel's Great Western Railway Bill was passed into law in 1835. The line was opened to Maidenhead in 1838 and two years later reached Reading. Whilst the non-tidal river was given a new lease of life when the Thames Conservancy took over in 1866, rebuilding the older locks, removing some old flash locks and implementing a continuous programme of shoal dredging, competition from the railway caused long distance traffic to decline drastically. Lost revenues by way of tolls from loaded barges caused both the Kennet and Avon Canal and the Thames and Severn Canal to go into steep decline. By the 1880s, a mere handful of barges were passing through these waterways. Nevertheless on the Thames itself, in 1905, over 70,000 tons was carried above Staines, much of it going to and from associated waterways like the Wey Navigation and the Oxford Canal. A considerable amount was made up of fairly localized horsedrawn barge traffic on the higher reaches, like the carriage of grain grown in the Vale of the White Horse to Reading, from the wharves at Sutton Courtenay in Oxfordshire.

The mechanical age had by now reached far up the river in the form of steam tugs and barges. Tugs quickly replaced both the need for a sail and bowhauling by horses, and by the late nineteenth century they were regularly towing strings of dumb (engineless) barges up to Oxford. Steam barges in service in the 1920s carried 50-ton loads of grain from the London docks to various upriver mills, sometimes with a backload of beer from Simmond's Brewery at Reading. Raw materials such as rags for papermaking were brought by barge to Taplow, Temple and other paper mills. Imported grain went to corn mills at Marsh and Sonning. In spite of competition from the railways, in the 1920s the Thames Conservancy annual merchandise figures for traffic above Teddington amounted to some 350,000 tons.

Steel barges under tow regularly delivered hundreds of tons of imported timber – ranging from exotic hardwoods from Africa and the Indies to pitch pine from the Baltic regions – to the timber yards that lined the river banks at Kingston, Marlow, Reading and Oxford. Much of this timber was loaded in the Surrey Commercial Docks, which handled a large amount of barge traffic because there was no railway access to the site. The tugs had quite comfortable living accommodation, sufficient for a week away from home, and the Dutch-built lighters had cramped quarters in the stern where a lighterman or two might sleep overnight.

By the end of World War II, river traffic was in terminal decline for any number of reasons, largely due to increasing competition from road transport, but also resistance in the port by dockers and lightermen to new working practices. Nevertheless the average of about 300,000 tons per annum was maintained right up to the 1950s.

In March 1952 the firm of Becketts took its last 100-ton barge load of grain to Sonning Mill.[14] Maintenance closures to locks which closed the river to through traffic for three months meant that the mill had to bring in road transport. They found it much more economical and the lorries stayed. Thereafter there was a very rapid decline in freight movement above Teddington and in 1972 the merchandise figures barely reach 4,000 tons for the whole year.

It seems fitting that traffic on the Thames above London should end, as it began, still carrying its two most significant commodities: grain and wood. Cereals and timber had been sent downstream by barge for nearly two thousand years, keeping the population of London warm and fed. The same products, which now came to the Port of London from all around the world, were making the same journey, along the same river, in much the same craft, only now in reverse.

The decline and eventual demise in waterborne traffic on the Thames can be attributed to many things. Though often blamed on labour relations within the Port of London and the forceful doggedness with which the dockers and lightermen held onto their work in the face of change and modernization, this was not the reason, rather it was their response to global changes in shipping goods, better, faster, cheaper transport systems, new technology and the changing needs of people, over which they had no control.

Though two world wars slowed down the inevitable end, they also created the circumstances for transformation. Post-war Britain was a very different country; London destroyed and its population decimated were events equally as catastrophic as the Black Death or the Great Fire. Yet in a similar fashion, such huge catastrophes cleared the way, along with the wartime rubble and debris, for a coming generation with innovative ideas and fresh ways of doing things.

Alhough the Thames was no longer the vital artery which had

once provided London with its daily bread, in spite of the changes that had been wrought on the capital, its river and its waterborne freight traffic, grain continued to be barged along the Thames for a few more years yet. The story was not quite ended.

Nineteenth and Twentieth Century
Bread Recipes

In 1822 Maria Eliza Rundell suggested that her bread roll recipe was just as good as that found at Sally Lunn's in Bath, which is quite the claim as Sally Lunn's highly popular bun achieved legendary status in its day. You can judge for yourself however, as Sally's buns can still be enjoyed at her old house in Bath.

RUNDELL'S BREAD ROLLS

Warm one ounce of butter in half a pint of milk, put to it a spoonful and a half of yeast of small beer, and a little salt. Put two pounds of flour into a pan and mix in the above. Let it rise an hour; knead it well; make into seven rolls, and bake in a quick oven. If made in cakes three inches thick, sliced and buttered, they resemble Sally Lumm's, as made at Bath. The foregoing receipt, with the addition of a little saffron boiled in half a tea-cupful of milk, makes them remarkably good.[15]

POTATO BREAD

The recipe Elizabeth David gives in her *English Bread and Yeast Cookery* is a nineteenth century one. It is from a book called *Receipts in Modern Cookery,* published in 1805 by Dr A. Hunter, who describes his potato bread in the following words:

The lovers of toast and butter will be much pleased with this kind of bread. The potato here is not added with a view to economy, but to increase the lightness of the bread, in which state it will imbibe the butter with more freedom.[16]

The original recipe called for fresh yeast. This one has been adapted to use fast action yeast, so that it can be added directly to the flour and only requires one rising rather than two.

Ingredients:
450 g (1 lb) strong white bread flour
1-2 medium potatoes (enough to yield about 120 g (4 oz) of cooked, mashed potato)
140 ml (½ cup) milk
140 ml (½ cup) water
2 teaspoons ground sea salt
1 x 7 g (¼ oz) sachet fast action / easy blend yeast

Scrub the potatoes and leave the skins on. Put the potatoes in a saucepan and pour over boiling water adding a good pinch of salt. Cover the saucepan and cook the potatoes until just fork tender – 20 minutes or more, depending on size. Once cooked, drain off the water, cover the potatoes with a thick, clean cloth, put the lid back on the pan and leave them for a few minutes. Peel the potatoes as soon as they can be handled. Break them into chunks and place in a sieve or potato ricer. Sieve them so they are without lumps. You need about 120 g of sieved potato. Set aside but keep warm.

Combine the flour, salt and yeast in a large, warm mixing bowl. Add the still warm sieved potato to the flour and, using your hands, rub the potatoes into the flour so that they are thoroughly mixed. Make a warm mixture of milk and water by combining about 90 ml of boiling water with 50 ml of cold water and add this to about 140 ml of cold milk. Make a well in the centre of the flour and pour in the water and milk mixture. Mix to form a soft dough with your hands. If it feels too wet and sticky, sprinkle with some more flour. Knead the dough on a floured surface for about 10 minutes or until smooth and elastic (or use a mixer and dough hook for about 5 minutes).

Now shape the dough as desired. For a single loaf, place the dough into a warmed and greased loaf tin (about 2.5 to 3 pint capacity), or shape into about 8 roughly equal-sized rolls and place on a warmed, greased baking tray.

Cover with a damp cloth and leave to rise until about doubled in bulk (this will take longer than for ordinary yeast bread, anything up to two hours). The use of a damp cloth is important, as this dough tends to form a skin, which can inhibit rising when put in the oven and makes for a tougher crust.

Bake in a hot oven (220°C / 425°F / Gas 7) for about 35 to 45 minutes for a single loaf and 15 to 20 minutes for rolls. The bread should make a hollow sound when tapped. Don't let the crust get too browned or hard.

THE NATIONAL LOAF

The National Loaf was a bread made from wholemeal flour with added calcium and vitamins, introduced in Britain during World War II. In order to combat wartime shortages of white flour, it was made from wholemeal flour. A dirty grey in colour, the National Loaf was unpopular with a population used to white bread. It quickly gained the nickname 'Hitler's secret weapon'.[17] Eleanor Roosevelt, the American First Lady, noted on a visit to Buckingham Palace in 1942 that 'We were served on gold and silver plates, but our bread was the same kind of war bread every other family had to eat.'[18]

Ingredients:
600 g (1½ lb) national flour (wholemeal with 15 percent potato flour)
1 ½ tablespoons salt (this is a LOT but it helped to preserve it)
1 ½ tablespoons dried yeast
1 dessertspoon shoney or treacle
450 ml (2 cups) tepid water with ½ vitamin C tablet dissolved

Mix together all the ingredients and knead for about 10 minutes until you have a soft dough. Place the dough in an oiled bowl, cover with a tea towel and leave until dough has doubled in size (around two hours).

Knock back the dough, give a short knead then cut into two equal pieces. Place in 1½ litre loaf tins, allow to rise for a further two hours.

Preheat oven to 200°C / 440°F / Gas 6. Bake loaves for 30 minutes. To test the loaves turn them out of their tins and give the base a tap, if it sounds hollow they are ready. Allow to cool on a wire rack.

Chapter Thirteen

Life on the Barges

We once worked barges taking grain from Tilbury Grain Terminal to Coxes Mill on the River Wey. Coxes Mill closed in 1983 and with its closure the last regular upriver freight traffic on the Thames from the London docks finally ceased. The mill too has gone, now converted into trendy apartments obliterating the last traces of a particular way of life, indeed many ways of life, lives overtaken by changes unforeseen. Gone are most of the skills of those who built the boats, the bargemen who brought the grain, the millers who ground the corn, and the men and women who baked the bread that fed the people. The story of all those individuals is encapsulated in the story of the Wey. To mark its role, and before memory blurs, it is worth recounting briefly the story of the Wey Navigation and recalling the lives of those who worked upon it, including my own.

The Wey, in commercial terms, outlasted many of its counterparts. It was one of the earliest navigations to install pound locks and was a wide and easily maintained waterway with a good water supply. On 26 June 1651 an Act of Parliament was granted to 'Guildford Corporation and others to make the Wey [between Guildford and Weybridge] navigable at their own expense'.[1] Shares were sold and capital raised. The Wey Navigation consisted of a man-made canal and adapted (dredged and straightened) parts of the River Wey. One of the first inland waterways in Britain, it was completed in just two years and comprised nine miles of canalised river, with twelve locks and twenty bridges. It cost only £16,000 (about £1 million today) to build, yet it was dogged for many years by problems caused by financial difficulties. A second Act of Parliament passed in 1661 handed control of the waterway to six trustees. Slowly the Navigation prospered, as did Guildford, the main town on the waterway. Barge traffic steadily increased with many goods being sent from there to London. By the 1720s the Wey Navigation carried an average of 17,000 tons of produce per year, generating about £2,000 in revenue from its tolls.

Although not the first man-made navigation to be constructed, (the River Lea has that distinction), it was certainly the largest and the first commercially viable waterway in the land. Effectively preceding the so-called 'Canal Age' by at least a hundred years, it provided a wealth of proven practices for later canal builders and was the model that encouraged a flurry of waterway building activity across England.

The river empties into the Thames at Weybridge, which is some 31 miles from London Bridge. First accounts of barges working between the Wey Navigation and London date from 1653. Over the course of time a rich variety of goods was hauled up and down the river. Cargoes variously included timber, sugar, maize and barley, oil-cake, kapok, linseed, gunpowder, bricks, coal for the local gas-works, chalk and bark for the flourishing tanneries, rags for papermaking, barrel hoops, and at the end of World War I even surplus fighter aircraft were moved by barge. There were more mills per mile along the Wey than anywhere else in Britain, with the mill at Coxes Lock near Addlestone in Surrey being the largest. At one point the main river powered twenty-two mills. Not surprising, then, that the most regular and constant of loads should be corn, shipped to the abundant flour mills which stretched along its full length, and the milled flour often providing a useful backload for the journey back down to London. In *A Tour Thro' the Whole Island of Great Britain*, Daniel Defoe, who lived in the Wey Valley, recorded that corn bought at the corn market in Farnham was transported to the mills on the river, and then shipped to London by barge once it had been processed.[2]

Promotional postcard for Coxes Lock Mill.

Barges from Wm. Stevens & Sons in Thames Lock, Wey Navigation, taking grain from Surrey Docks to Coxes Lock Mill.

Life on the Barges

From the 1840s, specialized Wey barges were being built in Guildford by the firm of William Stevens & Sons. They were capable of carrying 80 tons of freight and were the embodiment of centuries of knowledge concerning the craft of wooden barge-building and, equally importantly, a thorough understanding of the work such craft were designed to do. Built with elm bottoms, oak sides, pitch pine kelsons and iron knees, they were strong and long-lasting. Flat-bottomed with an overall length of 73 feet 3 inches and a width of 13 feet 8 inches, their very specific dimensions were tailor-made to fit the locks of the Basingstoke Canal and the Wey Navigation, through which they must regularly pass. Their straight-sided hulls were held rigid by tension chains and crossbeams.

Once loaded with loose or bagged grain, fitted hatch boards with a final spread of tarpaulins covered the hold, keeping the grain dry as it made its way up the river. A barrel windlass was set low on the foredeck, there to raise and lower the anchor when needed on the tideway, and sometimes to be called into play to warp the barge alongside ships in the busy London docks. The transom stern was flat and the large wooden rudder which hung off the back was hinged and held with a pin. In the locks, it could be swung flush with the stern so as not to foul on gates and cills. The removable tiller, like the windlass, was set low, close to the deck, with a lower section of deck where the bargemaster would stand to steer his craft. In the 1880s, some carried small spritsails to aid navigation on the Thames, but usually horses were hired to tow them as far as Putney. From there, tugs would be used to take them up and down the tideway.

The 'western' barges frequently had to rest overnight in the London docks, often loading late at night or in the early morning. Tide and tugs worked a different timetable to that of the rest of the world and craft needed to be manned in readiness. The Wey barges were equipped with a small cabin located under the stern deck. Fitted out with two bunks, built-in cupboards and an iron stove, this was home to the men when they had to stay on board.

By the 1920s, William Stevens & Sons barges were carrying cargoes of maize loaded from Canadian ships in the Surrey Commercial Docks up to Coxes Mill at Weybridge, and bringing away flour. The barge book of 1935, which recorded details of all barges transiting Thames Lock, the first lock where the Wey joins the Thames, shows that two of Stevens' barges were regularly passing through, each loaded with 80 tons of wheat for Coxes Mill. By then, the only other freights coming onto the Wey were coal for Woking gasworks (though this finished with its closure in 1939), timber (which was also destined for Woking and which finished in 1949 with the closure of the canal), and imported linseed grains for Ham Mills. This traffic ceased in 1963 when the mills burnt down. After that the only trade left was the carriage of grain from the London docks to Coxes Mill at Addlestone.

William Stevens & Sons were not only barge builders, but would later become the prime carriers on the river. According to David Rose, in his 'Life on the Wey Navigations', the family's long connection with the canal trade can be traced back to William Stevens (1777-1856), a carpenter by trade:

> In 1822 [William] secured the important job as lock keeper at Thames Lock, Weybridge, where he learned to make accurate records of the cargoes being transported on the waterway. Three years later he became wharfinger at Guildford. His eldest son, also named William (1810-1890), became a carpenter and by 1840 had built his own barge, *Perseverance,* and was trading on the navigation.
>
> By 1847, William II had a new barge, *Reliance,* and by 1857 owned three more and had seven men working for him. He had been employed part-time by his father as assistant wharfinger at Guildford and after his father had died, took up the position full-time. He too named his first son William (1844-1936), and like his father and grandfather before him he too trained as a carpenter, and with his brother John, joined their father's business.[3]

This William became general manager of the Godalming Navigation in 1869, and began to buy shares in it in 1888. On his father's death two years later, William became the manager of the

Life on the Barges

20 mile stretch of the Wey Navigation, which ran from Godalming to Weybridge. He sought to ensure ownership and in 1889 he and his brother bought up most of the shares. By the 1890s, William Stevens & Sons had a fleet of eight barges and a monopoly of the Wey Navigation. Finally, in 1902, they gained overall financial ownership of the waterway and received the majority of the tolls. The company was flourishing; as well as barges, it also ran a successful coal merchant's business, undertook marine civil engineering work and operated steam tugs on the River Thames.[4]

The coming of the railways in the 1840s marked the onset of rapid decline for many canals. Stevens & Sons was instrumental in keeping the Wey Navigation open, even at a time when the railways were rapidly transforming the way goods were moved around the country. On the Wey, corn mills continued to transport their grain and flour by boat, although tonnage fell from a peak of 86,003 tons in 1838 to 24,581 tons in 1890. The Stevens family fought to maintain the Navigation and from 1890 to 1910 traffic rose again to over 30,000 tons, with a rise to 51,115 tons in 1918. In 1912 the then current William Stevens went to court to transfer the powers of the Wey Trustees to his family who, in effect, became the owners and managers of the Navigation as well as the main carriers. The family's fleet of barges helped to maintain trade at a healthy level between 1918 and 1939. They were the last owners of the Wey Navigation.[5]

Luckily for us life on the barges is well documented in a little book called *Captain White's River Life*. As a bargemaster working for William Stevens, Captain White recounts in some detail what life was like on working barges at the time. Asked what was the longest single trip he had ever done, he replied:

> We went down to London on the first of the month and finished the trip on the last of the month. We were waiting for cargo. We would go to a wharf, pick up about five or ten ton, then you'd go to a dock for what we called 'cotchels' – a little bit here and a little bit there. Sweepings [of grain] off a ship or out of a warehouse – say a few hundredweight. We'd go to all the different docks until we had a full freight which would be

about seventy or eighty tons. Well, you'd get back to the mill and then you'd have to unload all these different little 'cotchels' – where they had come from – you'd have a big pile of papers that you'd signed for and in the meantime – you'd come from London to Coxes…to Weybridge…Perhaps half of it had been sold to Bowyers of Stoke Mill. Then all these papers had to be lined up, re-signed again…oh, it used to be a paraphernalia! But sometimes with timber too. We'd go to a dock and load about fifty tons of maize, or fifty tons of barley or oats – well then they'd send you to a timber dock. You may load about six to ten standards of timber – on top of your hatches and everything. Well then when you got to Weybridge you had to unload the timber into another barge, all for nothing – you didn't get paid for doing that. That all comes in your freight. P'raps you'd get ninepence or a shilling a ton – that's all you had. And your actual money was only twenty-three [pounds] and six [shillings] per week. Well it was a lot of money in those days.[6]

He goes on to describe other elements of the bargeman's life:

When you got to the dock, p'raps you'd lay outside the dock for eight or nine hours. The docks used to be so busy in those days. And when you did get into the dock, p'raps you had to go from the Albert dock to the Victoria dock to a place called 'the silos' for the next morning's work. 'Cause if you didn't get there ready to start at eight o'clock you didn't get anything that day. No – they put someone else in your place. Then when you finished loading in there, you had to row all the way back…and you were loaded then…So if you got a headwind, it was just too bad. But more or less, we used to get tows up and down [the docks], you know. We used to be well known up on the river and in the docks.

Trying to envisage rowing a barge loaded with some 80 tons of grain is hard enough, even more so Captain White's description of unloading a barge of its grain. Until the arrival of the bulk carriers,

Life on the Barges

grain was still bagged in the traditional 'quarter' sacks. He describes how they used to unload them at certain mills on the Wey:

> When they used to come up with the barge, they used to put two long planks alongside each other [from the barge to the bank], and I've known my dad…I never did it…I couldn't do it…used to carry two and a half hundredweight on his back up out of the barge, along the planks and onto the shore.

These same size sacks had been the standard quarter since medieval times, and men loading and unloading ships had to carry these huge weights upon their backs, just as Captain White's father did.

When loaded, the side-decks of these old wooden barges were almost submerged. Once under tow, especially with a tug skipper more used to towing Thames lighters tight up behind him which needed no steering, the hapless bargemaster was at the mercy of the tug driver. Captain White recounts just such an occasion when the loaded barge he was steering was being towed upstream from London to Teddington:

> I had a tug called the *Scorcher* and the skipper that was on it at the time, he didn't care if he pulled you under water or not. And we went up Syon Reach and the barge took a run – started to run. I couldn't control it. One end of the tow rope was on the tug; the other was on the bitt-heads. I couldn't let any more out, and that was – oh – a good eight fathom. Because the further away you were from the tug the better it was to steer. But this barge, she was a marvelous barge for keeping a dry deck, but this day she didn't. And she took a dive, so her head went under water; she took a dive and a run for the bank. We ran up on the foreshore and it went right over – half under water on one side – and went straight along the foreshore… came off afloat again!…Didn't do any damage. But my heart was in my mouth! I thought to myself, I'm going to have to swim now! He never stopped, never even eased up.

It is clear from Captain White's account that the skills of a bargeman went far beyond the ability to simply steer his barge. He needed to know his craft intimately, its merits and its shortcomings. These barges, the last of which were built in the 1940s, were still working up and down the tideway and in out of the docks until the 1960s. Even on the quieter reaches above Teddington Lock hazards presented themselves. One of the worst was the weir pool immediately before the entrance to the Wey itself. Here Captain White describes how the tug had to manoeuvre itself in order to safely pull its charges across this dangerous stretch of river, a place of conflicting currents which in times of flood became a whirlpool, a maelstrom of white water.

Just below Thames Lock, Harmsworth's used to have a wharf there below the stop lock. There's a tin shed on there – well, that's where they used to do a lot of repairs and unloading there – coal to go to Woking and turn timber over to smaller boats to Guildford – and all that kind of thing. Used to be just room in there to swing a tug. And when you went in there in a flood you used to go in there full pelt, full on, to pull the second barge in out of the weir. Well, you've got the River Wey this side, you've got the weir there and that's how it's going, right the way round all the time. And then you've got the back weir as well, from the Thames and that's coming down all the time. But there's only one way to get out past the weir onto the Thames. You've got two streams. You had to go into that stream and as your head turned, so you let it go into the other stream and as soon as the tug got out of that stream, you put everything on, so's the barges wouldn't go and hit the towpath. I've seen tow ropes break – barges piled up there…oh dear, oh dear…! I've seen a barge sunk there – ran into a tug and sunk there. Got into the whirlpool…Couldn't get out, then all of a sudden she comes out…Hits the tug…shoved her right bang up onto the bank. But if you judge it right you can go straight out.

Just as during the time of the Black Death when London was

so beset, throughout two world wars the bargemen continued their work with the same dogged determination, moving grain, flour and other products from the docks to where they were needed. Captain White's recollection of his time on barges during World War II reflects this pragmatic approach: 'You just got on and did it,' he said.

When asked if there was much traffic on the river during the war, he answered:

There were hundreds and thousands of barges, tugs, ships – soon as the ships came in they worked day and night till they finished unloading, then away again. Oh, there were wrecks everywhere in London, in the docks, up and down the river. You had to wait for the convoys to come in. Well, when the convoys come in you darned well knew that London was going to get a beating. We loaded one Sunday, about five of our barges in the West India Dock with grain, and we were all loaded, then about the third ship from us…all of a sudden it just erupted… aerial torpedo had come up…sptt!

I was in Poplar Dock one time. I came into the dock somewhere around 11 o'clock at night. I'd gone from the West India Dock rowed my barge round into Poplar to be the next one loaded with coal. They used to load you in twenty minutes…they used to shoot it straight out of the trucks, straight into the barge. Black everywhere! And I'd got the barge alongside the chute and I thought to myself…well I dunno…I'll leave it till the morning. I'd just got down into the cabin…I'd made myself a cup of tea…bang! I was in the water! One barge lost!

Another time, they dropped an incendiary straight through the deck into my cupboards. Blew me out of the hatch. I lived up to my name then…I was white…all white…as if somebody had thrown a bucket of whitewash over me. I spent the night walking about. I see a policeman…course he came and grabbed me, walking about in the dock a bit on the dazed side. He took me to a big underground shelter. The next day I went to look

at my barge and there it was – sticking up out of the water…
what was left of it. They gave me a traveling ticket and I came
home. Then I had trouble with my back…started to itch
and scratch…went up to the hospital and they found I'd all
incendiary particles in my back and bottom. So I had to go in
hospital under what they called an electro-magnet to pull 'em
out. I was in there for about three weeks.

His recollections of the war come thick and fast, including
being strafed by a German aircraft as they went down the Wey.
Captain White was on board steering his barge, which was loaded
with tree trunks bound for the Regent's Canal Dock at Limehouse.
The barge was being towed by a horse.

This Jerry came over…he machine-gunned the barge…we
seen the bullets going into the logs. Old Len Turner, who was
leading the horse, he dived into the ditch…'Course you wasn't
troubled about your horse, was you? He said, well if he's had
it, he's had it, same as me. Couldn't do much about it! Well I
was watching this bloke come down…I could see what he was
going to do…he was going to machine-gun the barge from end
to end. Anyway the bullets went all alongside the barge, right
along, then he went. I could see some ack-ack and then some
aircraft…I suppose some of ours after him. That same trip we
got to Paddington on the Saturday afternoon and Saturday
night they emptied the canal. They dropped bombs all the
way along the canal…emptied it. So we were like that. [He
inclines his hand.] We couldn't lay in our bunks…we had to go
ashore…couldn't get home.
    I was jolly glad when the war finished anyway.

Captain White came from a long line of upriver bargemen. His
grandfather died in 1905, the year that Captain White was born.
He started working with his bargemaster father at the age of twelve
and was fully employed as the 'cabin boy' on barges with his father
and a mate from the age of fourteen. Fifty years later in 1969 he

and his barge *Perseverance* delivered the last load of grain carried by Wm. Stevens & Sons before the company finally ceased trading. Work on the Thames was steadily disappearing and on the Wey all trade other than that to Coxes Mill had gone. As is often the case, a number of discrete elements in combination conspired to bring about the end of the long association between the company of Wm. Stevens & Sons and the mill beside Coxes Lock.

The Wey Navigation itself was in need of ongoing maintenance and dredging, but there were no longer any toll payments or barge profits to pay for it. During the 1960s, the London docks, where Stevens' barges habitually loaded, were steadily closing and the Port of London Authority was extending dock facilities down at Tilbury. In 1969 the new grain terminal at Tilbury was completed. Improved rail loading facilities at Tilbury had enabled British Rail to undercut both the existing waterborne traffic and road transport as well. The wooden Wey barges were ageing and without engines; the distance to travel was further and they would have been particularly vulnerable loading down at Tilbury. The cards were stacked against continuing. Thus came the end of an era for Wm. Stevens & Sons, an era which had spanned more than two hundred years. British Rail built a spur line which allowed wagons full of imported grain to be loaded at Tilbury and delivered directly to Coxes Mill.

Once the decision was made that barge traffic to Coxes Mill was to cease, the Wey Navigation as a commercial proposition was clearly no longer viable. In 1964 Harry Stevens relinquished the canal and entrusted its safekeeping in perpetuity to the National Trust. It became the official owner in 1971.[7]

But, as it happened, this was not to be quite the end of commercial carrying on the river.

The story of Coxes Mill is inextricably bound up with the carriage of grain by water. Mill and waterway enjoyed a positive, symbiotic relationship for more than two hundred years, and in the main, the millers, carriers and owners of the Wey had common cause and little reason to change the status quo. Where raw materials could be shipped directly from source (or in the case of imported goods from the destination port), without need for double-handling, to the place where they would be processed, all other things being equal the transport of such goods by water remained an option. Grain to Coxes was a good example. It had little reason not to receive its imported grain by water for as long as there were men and barges to carry on the trade, and a viable waterway on which to do it.

The original Coxes Mill was built in 1776 by a Mr Cox, an iron manufacturer. When it finally closed on 8 April 1983, it had operated as a mill in various guises for over two hundred years and was the last commercially operated mill in Surrey. Water mills, by virtue of their simple technology, could be put to all sorts of uses. Coxes Mill for example was not only used for the manufacture of iron, but also, more surprisingly, for silk weaving. Coxes converted to flour production in the 1830s and this remained its principal focus until it closed. Unlike many of the mills further upstream, Coxes Mill continued to be a very successful operation, able to invest in new machinery and, perhaps more importantly, in new technology. The mill was rebuilt in 1901 and extended in 1906. It became one of the most important industrial buildings in the country at that time.

Sadly the same innovatory drive for modernisation, coupled with the development of more powerful engines, heralded the end of water power for the mill. It switched first to steam power and then later to electricity. Machinery which could suck grain directly out of the barge holds replaced the earlier slower manhandling methods. By the mid-1960s a new wheat holding silo some 137 feet (42 metres) in height was erected and later, in 1969, another was built to hold flour.[8]

Captain White's account of the mill's latter-day history is somewhat garbled but makes a good story. He tells it like this:

> Just after I started, Bowyers mill finished. The big mills were starting to spring up, taking the work from them, same as Coxes. Coxes had to expand you see. Well then, Coxes was taken over by the Allied Mills. That's a big Canadian firm. There's a little bit of a tale to that, too. Because, during the war

he sent a million ton of flour over here – cor, what's the name of the feller – I forget their name now – they used to make a biscuit before the war and send it over here. Churchill said that when the war was over he'd let him come over here and start his business. Well, when the war was finished Churchill wouldn't let him, he said, well, I will get over there – and he did. He got in. Married the wife of one of the main directors…'cause he'd died you see, and left her in with a few other shareholders…took her shares over…and of course, that's how they got hold of the place. Now he's got the big monopoly over in this country now.

The Coxes Lock Milling Company appears to have been a family run business from the late 1900s onwards. It has proved difficult to find out anything much about its ownership until the early 1960s when it was, seemingly, taken over by Allied Mills. Captain White's account may give some clue to the mystery. Curiously, the real story concerning the final owners of Coxes Mill is another family saga detailing an astonishingly rapid rise 'from rags to riches'. It is also a story which encapsulates the fate of bread in an increasingly industrialized world where profit had become paramount. Predicated upon a noble premise, that of putting a readily affordable loaf of good white bread on the table of even the poorest of individuals, the result was to be a pre-sliced, plastic encased travesty which has since dominated the British market for some eighty years.

George Weston, born in 1864, the son of English immigrants, was still a boy, just twelve years old, when he was apprenticed to a Toronto baker. In 1882, George went into business for himself when he bought a bread route from his employer a few years later. His business prospered and two years later he bought his former employer's bakery. Some time later he recalled those early days: 'I baked 250 loaves the first day. I delivered them – drove my own wagon – called on every customer myself.'[9]

With one old wood-burning oven and two young journeyman bakers, he developed his Real Home-Made Bread loaf. He used the best of ingredients, namely Manitoba No.1 hard wheat and Ontario fall wheat, combined 'in about equal proportion'. As his bread became increasingly popular, he expanded his premises. He began introducing the latest equipment to modernize the baking process, such as mechanical mixers to prepare the dough. By the 1890s, he had renamed his bakery G. Weston's Bread Factory. Although the latest machinery and a bigger bakery made for a more efficient operation, George attributed his success to one thing: 'Merit did it – the merit of my bread. You won't find any better bread made than mine. Folks all like it. Every year adds new customers.'[10]

In 1897, his Toronto-based modern bread factory, which he called the Model Bakery, was turning out 20,000 loaves a week. Soon he was baking some thirty types of bread with his 'Real Home-Made Bread' product remaining the most popular. By the turn of the century he had become Canada's biggest baker.

When war came to Europe, much to the worry of George and his wife Emma Maud, their eldest son volunteered for duty with the Canadian Expeditionary Force. But his father refused to allow him to join up and put him to work in his biscuit factory, cleaning and repairing equipment. In 1917, having reached the legal age for enlistment, just a few weeks before his nineteenth birthday, W. Garfield Weston enlisted in the Canadian army. He had his share of harrowing experiences on the front lines in France but returned from the war unscathed. Unscathed, but full of ideas based on things he had seen – he proposed that the company import biscuit-making equipment from England so that the biscuits made there could be manufactured and sold in Canada. The result was the successful launch of Weston's English Quality Biscuits in 1922.

In 1924, on the death of his father, Garfield followed in his footsteps and became president of George Weston Limited. In 1929, the stock market crashed, businesses failed and unemployment skyrocketed. In spite of the 'Great Depression' the company continued and successfully acquired a string of bakeries. Canada's wheat farmers were among the hardest hit at the time with incomes dropping by 75 percent. As the international markets dried up, so did the fields of Canadian farmers. The collapse in the price of wheat, combined with drought, devastated thousands of farming

Life on the Barges

families. Garfield Weston had an idea: he thought that he could increase demand for the country's wheat by establishing a chain of bakeries in Great Britain. He was convinced he could produce a better loaf of bread using more Canadian wheat, and in the process expand an important overseas market to the benefit of the country's grain farmers. In the midst of the depression he managed to convince an American, Ben Smith, a renowned speculator, to risk investing in his idea. They shook hands and looking him in the eye, Garfield said, 'I'll make you a lot of money.'[11]

He soon acquired the business of a failing biscuit manufacturer in Scotland, closed it down and moved production to a new facility in Edinburgh. With modern machinery he could produce high quality low cost biscuits which were soon selling at half the price of his competitors. Next he began buying up bread companies. By 1935 he had purchased a string of bread and biscuit plants throughout England, Ireland and Scotland. In addition to modernizing equipment and facilities he began making better quality bread by using more Canadian wheat. 'I want to give the public the best quality bread that can be produced...I hope at the same time to increase the demand for Canadian wheat, which is the best in the world, as you know, and which makes a better bread than any other.'[12]

Garfield tried to convince other British firms to use more Canadian wheat, but with limited success. It is here that Captain White's account, probably picked up as gossip as he was unloading his barge at Coxes Mill, begins to have some relevance. It seems likely that having been unable to persuade others to use more of his country's wheat, the most obvious answer as far as Garfield was concerned was for him to import it himself.

He called his company Food Investments Limited; it was originally incorporated in 1935, then almost immediately changed its name to Allied Bakeries and thereafter rapidly expanded with major interests in bakery. Unable to source flour of the right quality, quantity and price, Garfield Weston proceeded to buy up many small independent millers in the UK.

While Garfield built new factories, his basic strategy was

to acquire established companies through friendly merger and acquisition. Time and again he approached the heads of family-run firms. Many had been in the same business for generations but were now losing money; with deference and respect, he asked them to join him. I believe that this must have been what happened to Coxes Mill, and Captain's White version of events is probably not too far from the truth.

Allied Bakeries probably bought the Coxes Lock Milling Company, a family business, in the late 1930s or early 1940s, leaving the incumbents and their company name in place to continue running the mill, but now supplying it with Canadian hard wheat.

In the four years since he'd bought his first bakery in Britain, Garfield had succeeded in mass-producing an English biscuit everybody could afford. At the same time he was importing more Canadian hard wheat, which was to the benefit of the Canadian farmer and making a better British loaf of bread. Now, at age 39, Garfield Weston headed Allied Bakeries, employing over 5,000 workers at 15 plants and was hailed in the press as 'Britain's biggest baker'.[13]

Even while he made his mark in business, Garfield Weston had an interest in politics. He settled in Britain and in November 1939 became the Member of Parliament for the working class constituency of Macclesfield. Two months previously, Britain had declared war on Nazi Germany; Weston's contribution was to be less in the House than in rallying support for the war effort, particularly in helping to feed Londoners during the Blitz. He knew Winston Churchill well.

In 1945 Garfield Weston's thoughts turned back to Canada. In two decades he had built a multinational enterprise that spanned the Atlantic; he was the British Empire's biggest baker. Now he felt it was time to leave politics and England and return to his homeland. Allied Bakeries was run in his stead by his son and continued to grow into a multimillion pound business empire.

In 1962 Allied Bakeries was renamed Associated British Foods and Allied Mills was one of its subsidiary companies. By 1964 Associated British Foods was the world's largest baker. Allied Mills, once part of the group then became Allied Mills Ltd, a division of ABF Grain Products Ltd. It was about this time that Coxes Mill, ceased to be known as the Coxes Lock Milling Company and became more obviously part of the Allied Mills group of mills.

When Coxes Mill joined Allied Mills it was milling 60 tonnes of flour each day. The production of five grades of white flour together with wheatmeal, wholemeal and bran was achieved by using the most modern milling machinery from Switzerland which utilized fluted steel rollers. However, Allied Mills owned a number of historic mills and recognized the efficiency and durability of older machinery. At Coxes Mill, its hundred year old belt-driven sifting machine continued to work happily alongside the newly installed stainless steel gadgetry.[14]

From its roots as a small Canadian bakery, the company founded by W. Garfield Weston in 1935 grew to become Britain's top manufacturer of bread, with more than one-third of the UK market. He achieved what he set out to do: opening up new markets for Canadian wheat farmers, and industrializing the bread making process to ensure that a good white loaf would grace the breakfast table of even the poorest family. By turning the world of bread making on its head he hastened the end of the traditional British baker. His bread factories, so ideally suited to incorporate the very latest developments in bread production, would ultimately lead to their demise. How contradictory it seems, then, that at the same time one of his companies should be instrumental in keeping alive an age-old transport system long after it had been abandoned by the rest of the world.

The Factory Loaf Recipe

In comparison with the grain of North America, wheat grown in Britain is soft and low in protein. British wheat, used on its own, is not particularly suitable for making the well-risen loaf of bread that most people prefer.

In 1961, the Chorleywood Bread Process (CBP) was developed, revolutionizing the way that bread is made. Significantly, it enabled bread produced in the UK to use the softer home grown wheats with a considerably lower protein content compared with the imported North American strong hard wheats. CBP has had a huge impact on the eating habits of the population so that today some 80 percent of the bread manufactured in the UK is produced by this method.[15] It is cheap, filling, soft, long-lasting and, because it can turn low-protein British wheat into palatable bread, a boon to British farmers.

CBP uses intensive high speed mixers to combine flour, improvers, vegetable fat, yeast and water to make dough, and the fermentation process is greatly speeded up. Solid fats are used to provide structure to the loaf during baking to prevent it collapsing. The whole process from flour to a ready loaf takes only 3 ½ hours. Two hours later it's ready to be sliced, packaged and distributed.

A typical recipe using CBP Bread Recipe would be:

100 kg (220 lbs) flour
2 kg (4 lbs) yeast
2 kg (4 lbs) salt
60.5 kg (132 lbs) water
1 kg (2 lbs) CBP improver
2 kg (4 lbs) hard fat

Don't try to bake this at home!

Chapter Fourteen

My Intrepid Story

As I have worked my way steadily through the story of grain transport on the Thames and its associated waterways I can't help but recall the way in which I was drawn, quite unconsciously, into becoming a minuscule part of its long history. Living on old barges whose trading life was over and moored against derelict wharves whose function was soon to be forgotten somehow made an unexplainable impression upon me. Unexplainable in the sense that other than being born in a Thames-side town and learning to swim in the river, I knew of no particular connection that I might have with waterways, its traffic or those who managed them. Yet I was drawn towards this life on the water, at first as an observer and later in ways far more involved.

In my teens, in the late 1950s, I lived for a while on a barge moored at the Hollows in Brentford, hard by the gasworks. I recall watching loaded lighters being guided by men using huge sweeps to steer the craft into the riverside wharves they were destined for. These ungainly swim-ended, engineless barges had hardly changed, other than in size, for centuries. They dominated the tidal river above and below London. In the 1950s there were still some 8,000 of them working on the water and at least 250 tugs. I remember the coal barges destined for Brentford Gasworks which had loaded from colliers berthed further downstream at Beckton, Nine Elms and Fulham. They came in a constant flow – towed up and down the river on every tide. The names of the lighterage firms that owned them, though long since gone, still roll easily off the tongue: Thames & General, Braithwaite & Dean, Clements Knowling, Clements Tough, Corys. The company name was written in large letters along the coamings on each side of the craft and on the tugs which towed them. They were a real fixture of river life and easily recalled some fifty or so years later. Just beyond where our barge was moored was a wharf owned by the Portland Cement Company, where the lighters unloaded bagged cement brought up from Essex. Occasionally, during the unloading, a bag would slip from the grasp of the crane, spilling its contents as it hit the ground; clouds of cement powder would darken the air. I can still recall the acrid taste it left in the mouth.

A little further upstream, loaded lighters owned by Thames & General, the largest lighterage company on the Thames, would be dropped off by the powerful tug which had towed them, six at a time, up from the London docks. This was at the entrance to the River Brent and Grand Union Canal. Lightermen would move effortlessly from barge to barge as they were gathered up, like a flock of wayward sheep, and towed by smaller tugs to the busy trading intersection that was the British Waterways Brentford Depot. It was there that two worlds met: the men of the tideway, with their clumsy lighters delivering imported goods from the London docks, and the canal boatmen, with their slender painted boats waiting to load and transport precious freight onwards to the interior of England, to manufacturing centres in the Midlands and beyond.

Wharves on the Thames, such as at the Hollows where we lived, were first recorded in the 1600s and ultimately lined the whole waterfront. Barges destined for such places had for centuries been rowed by lightermen using two great oars to control and steer their charges. They came up with the flood and went down on the ebb. Later, with the arrival of steam tugs, the lighters were towed, several at a time. On arrival at their various destinations they would be unloosed from the tug and rowed to shore by the two lightermen on board. It was a hugely skillful operation, requiring knowledge that no landsman could ever appreciate or instantly possess. The work of the lightermen was really only observed by the bystander when the weather was fine and a walk beside the river a pleasant undertaking.

My Intrepid Story

Few people, other than those who lived on the river, ever saw these same craft being worked in the dark, in fog or storms, or in winter ice and snow. Dangerous work it was, and a job handed down from father to son, whose education must, of necessity, take place out there on the water. Physically hard and unremitting, working the river – using the push of the current against the press of the tide and then allowing the calm of slack water to gently berth the barge – was a job requiring special skills which could take years to acquire. At the time, I had no idea what was involved. I was simply entranced by the slow, measured and silent movement of the lightermen as they went about their business.

Looking back, I realize that it was during this period living on what had once been a proud Thames sailing barge, now relegated to a slowly rotting houseboat, that I became aware of the river's working life, even if then it was for its more obviously romantic and dramatic elements. The look of the Thames barges moored nearby, their names alone – *The Lord Churchill, Brian Boru, Glencoe, Northumberland* and *Cumberland* – were enough to conjure fanciful dreams of sailing off down the river to destinations unknown. Interest in their history as craft, or their relationship with London, was to come rather later.

This was at a time when only one or two of these barges were still operating commercially. Fifty years earlier there were a couple of thousand working around our coasts and into the London docks; they were then as familiar a sight to Londoners as the red London bus today. In 1971, we were on board our own canal motor barge in the Regent's Canal Dock when the *Cambria*, the very last Thames barge to work entirely under sail, made her final journey up the Thames to St. Katherine's Dock. Such a sad day, but what a sight, and to think that this majestic vessel was no more than a humble carrier of cargo.

Little did I know then that only a few years later I would be used to working my way through the maze of lighters that clogged the entrance to the Brentford Depot and the Grand Union Canal in my own boat, or that the imported Canadian hard wheat arriving in the London docks, which I knew filled the holds of the laden barges and lighters heading upstream, would one day be loaded into craft of my own for a similar upriver destination.

Later, I moved onto the Grand Union Canal. There, for a number of years, my home was on an old canal barge moored near Uxbridge. It was here that we were drawn further and more intimately into the world of water-based freight carriage. The canal is physically much smaller than the Thames. Consequently, it was easier to get to know the people who worked the boats: the lightermen steering their barges laden with planks of teak and mahogany, loaded in Greenland Dock and destined for local canal-side timber yards; and the boatmen who worked their pairs of canal boats on the inland waterways that linked the south and the Midlands, carrying freight ranging from bricks to beer, bully beef to coffee beans, wheat and barley to coal and steel. These were very different tribes of men, whose only connection was that of being afloat. The worlds of bargemen, lightermen and canal boatmen, though overlapping, were not the same at all, and although some skills were common, the waters in which they worked and the type of craft they plied were quite different in detail to each other.

I recall while still in my teens going with my partner to find out about jobs that were being advertised to work on the canals. They wanted strong young couples, and training was to be given. Sadly, the need to advertise was a sign of the times, marking the inevitable drawing to a close of a particular way of life. Like the lightermen and sailing bargemen, the work of the canal boatmen had for generations been carried on in closed communities. Sons were expected to take up the trade of their fathers, as bargemasters and lightermen, and wives were mostly drawn from other families directly related to the work. This was also the case for the canal boatmen, though for reasons of economy their wives and family lived on board and were essentially the working crew. The nature of the work isolated them from daily life; few outsiders ever penetrated their world. It was not until the 1960s, when changes in working practices and in freight handling were drawing that world to a close, that it became possible for those of us 'off the bank' to taste something of the secret life of the boat people.

We went off to be interviewed at the British Waterways' Bulls

Bridge lay-by, near Hayes in Middlesex. This was a few miles above Brentford on the Grand Union Canal. It lay at another busy junction with the Paddington Arm, the branch off to London, which joined the Regent's Canal. The rivers Lea and Stort were here linked to the main Grand Union and its route to the Midlands and the north. Here was where the empty pairs of boats with their families on board waited for orders to load, the details of the freight and where it was to go.

Even today I can hear the tannoy booming out, calling boatmen to come to the office to collect the paperwork they needed. Orders on that particular day were for six pairs to go down to Brentford to load bulk grain destined for Whitworths Mill on the river Nene in Wellingborough, Northamptonshire, which had been shipping grain from London since 1887. We were shown the boats we might work – they came in pairs: one with an engine and the other, the 'butty', that was towed behind it. Between the two they could load about 50 tons of freight. I remember peering into the tiny stern cabins, one on each boat. This was where whole families, often quite large, lived full time. We were told that once we were skilled in the work, the two of us operating a pair of boats might earn as much as £14 a week. That, even then, was a tiny wage, especially in view of the long hours and heavy work involved. We declined the job and went busking in Paris instead. Yet only a few years later we were doing this very same work, albeit with our own pair of boats.

On our return from France, with little money and a developing penchant for doing our own thing, we moved from the river to the canal, where we bought an old wooden motor barge and set about converting it into a cruising home. It was on the old *Progress* that we learned how to handle a big boat and to cope with the problems of under-maintained waterways.

Sailing barges, narrowboats and London lighters, all were grist for my mill. Now, coming close to the end of their particular story after two thousand years or more, they nevertheless served to open a new chapter in my own.

Forced to look back on one's past life, the connections which went unconsidered at the time become clearer. Now, casting through all these memories, they seem too obvious to have been missed. That slight familiarity with river life gained from our time at the Hollows was enough: from old barges on the Thames to old barges on the canal was not such a big step to take – though the canal world turned out to be significantly different from that of the river.

The Thames was still all go then, a bustling, hustling environment of diesel tugs and unlovely lighters; a rough world sadly no longer redeemed by the presence of the elegant downriver sailing barges. The canal, when we first ventured upon it, seemed busy enough with traffic, but the trade, along with the waterway, was dying. Considered an anachronism since the coming of the railways and, later, an efficient road system, canal transport struggled to survive alongside its seemingly more effective competition. The 'painted boats' still went about their business, but on canals that were left undredged, with leaking locks and shallow pounds.

My visit to Bulls Bridge all those years ago gave me at least a slight understanding of the lives of the families who worked their pairs of boats up and down the country. Boatmen, generally illiterate, knew every inch of their routes and could recount a journey in detail, with the names of every lock and bridge, every straight and turn, every mooring deep enough for working boats to lie overnight, an oral litany learned as children and handed on to each subsequent generation. They went where their orders, to load or discharge, took them.

Unlike the nomadic gypsies they were often compared with, they travelled because their job required them to. Paid by the freight, if their boats weren't loaded they went hungry. The quicker they worked, the more freight they loaded, the more money they earned, though it was never a great deal. Life revolved totally around the canals they worked on, the wharves they tied at, the lock-side shops that provided their provisions, and the canal-side pubs where only boatmen drank. It was a closed world.

Viewed from the towpath, the passing boats so beautifully painted, with their shining brass portholes and decorative rope-work, it looked an idyllic life. Initially, it was probably this romantic view that attracted most 'outsiders' to life on the water. But it was hard, the hours were long, and during the winter working through locks in icy darkness was dangerous work. There could be no tying up just because the rain was lashing down or a blizzard was blowing, or even when there was sickness on board. Freight had to be delivered on time and new freight loaded.

I used to wave to the families from my window as they passed by, asking them where they were going and what they were carrying. Coal from the Midlands destined for the various mills and factories lining the canal banks; coffee beans for Hayes Cocoa loaded overside from foreign ships in the London docks; esparto grass to the John Dickinson paper mills in Hertfordshire; HP Sauce from Heinz at Harlesden heading down to the docks for export to who knows where. And wheat in huge quantities. Britain had long since ceased to be self-sufficient in wheat production and now relied on Russia, Canada, America and Australia to keep the country fed. Foreign-flagged grain ships now brought it to London where it was unloaded and stored in enormous granaries far down the river. Instead of loading wheat grown in the hinterlands of southern England and bringing it to London, barges now loaded imported wheat at Tilbury and carried it inland to modern flour mills. In 1959 the first motorway was opened in Britain; road rather than rail or water was fast becoming not only the chosen way to move produce, but eventually almost the only way. Flour was no longer bagged in friendly sacks destined for the village baker, but instead poured into huge tankers and delivered by road to the factories that now produced the bulk of Britain's bread.

Wheat loaded in London had been sent by canal boat to Whitworths Mill in Wellingborough for nearly a hundred years, but this came to an end in 1969. In the same year, the upriver traffic in grain from the London docks to Coxes Mill on the River Wey also ceased. True, imported wheat still arrived by ship, but the abiding link forged between the Thames and London by its grain traffic was weakening to the point of collapse.

Motivated partly by a real concern over the escalating disappearance of commercial craft from our rivers and canals, and perhaps a little beguiled by the romantic appeal of a boatman's life, sometime in the 1970s we sold the canal barge we had lived on for so many years and bought a working motor narrowboat. Noticing that a pair of boats, which regularly passed our houseboat home heading uphill loaded one day and running back light a day or two later, had ceased to come by, I contacted the British Waterways Board manager at the Brentford Depot to find out why. He explained that the boats we were used to seeing needed a lot of repairs and it was unlikely they would ever work again. I told him we had a good sound boat available, expecting him to want to hire it. Instead he said, 'Good, you be down here at 8 o'clock on Monday morning ready to load.' I put the phone down. As these canal boats worked as a pair and we only had the motor boat, we quickly arranged with a friend to borrow his 'butty' (the unpowered second boat towed by the motor boat), and somehow, in the moment, decided that this was an opportunity too good to miss. We would take the two boats to Brentford, as the manager had suggested.

Thus did our own first real involvement with working boats and barges begin. We had thought of ourselves as more than competent boaters, having travelled the Grand Union Canal between London and Birmingham many times and made frequent forays out onto the Thames in our dear old *Progress*. Working a pair of loaded boats, one towing the other, was an entirely different experience and we soon came to appreciate the skills of the born and bred boatmen as never before. That first journey, with overloaded boats, due to our lack of experience, took some thirty-six nonstop hours; a trip that a proper boatman and his wife could knock off in twelve. Luckily for us there were still a good number of these people left on the waterways and with the boats back in Brentford waiting to load on the Monday morning, every Sunday night was spent in The Brewery Tap, the boatman's pub by the lock.

Here, we would be regaled with accounts of heroic deeds and canal lore, and found the answers to all our questions about 'how to go on', as they called it. We learned the boatman's names for every lock and bridge, every turn and straight, as well as where the canal was so shallow we might run aground, or where it was deep enough for a pair of loaded boats to travel abreast or stop overnight.

My Intrepid Story

We learned how to work the pair efficiently through locks, how the boats should be loaded and what lines to tow with. Equally importantly, we were told where to find the best fish and chip shops in each town we passed through.

We slowly acquired the skills to do the job, discovering how to cope with empty pounds and leaking locks, to laboriously remove old mattresses or heavy tyres picked up by the boat's propellor, to work through locks where gates were jammed with rubbish, or worse still, in winter, with ice. All such hazards had to be dealt with, there was no one to call out to assist. Thus for several years during the 1970s, during the months of September to April, we carried regular loads of crude lime pulp, lime skins and occasionally lime oil, between Brentford and the L. Rose & Sons wharf at Boxmoor, on the Grand Union Canal. We found out what it was like to struggle through ice and snow, work through frozen locks in the dark, and to steer by the tops of trees in the frequently fog-bound Colne valley. How perverse, then, that this was a way of life we would come to love, no matter how hard the daily grind – though the sun did occasionally shine.

Our desire to get freight back onto the waterways sent us off in pursuit of ways and means. We formed a company, acquired premises and bought a few more working boats. We wrote to canal-side companies we knew who moved their goods through the docks, or received their raw materials from other river and canal-side sources. Many showed an interest, but with the few craft we now had available the logistics often simply would not work. This is something of a problem in any dying industry: when the infrastructure begins to fail and its various components disappear, there is a point where it cannot be re-established without some massive external event which demands a revival, as was the case with the two world wars. This was clearly illustrated in the world of waterways. Companies moved away from the riverside, no longer using coal to power their mills and factories, and turning to other forms of transport. Wharves were abandoned, cranes were sold for scrap, and no new craft built. The loss of specialist knowledge needed for working on the water and the traditional skills required to handle loaded barges was just part of the fallout; once it becomes redundant it is soon lost. Those jobs that survived the longest tended to have some special characteristic which made water transport the most practicable. In the case of Rose's lime juice and Coxes Mill grain, both companies received their basic commodity from overseas, in ships which docked in the Port of London; both companies carried out much of their operation from waterside premises on navigable waterways; both only required a certain amount of the essential product at any one time which could then be delivered in boat-size parcels. In the end, although Rose's and Coxes Mill have long since given up their waterside premises, the reasons for so doing were unrelated to their use of water transport.

Though hardly conscious of the ending of eras, the world in the 1950s and 1960s was changing fast. A post-war period of full employment as Britain rebuilt itself masked the real ending of the Industrial Revolution. Heavy industries were dying or leaving our shores. The Clean Air Acts of 1958 and 1963 sounded the death knell for the mainstay of canal transport – coal. Manufacturers ceased to use it, and with it the canal system. Motorways meant speedier transport and no need to double-handle goods. With better road communications, increased carrying capacity by heavy vehicles and the growth of containerization, each development brought the inevitable demise of inland water transport in Britain ever closer.

In truth, those of us battling to hold onto some waterborne trade were doing little more than fighting a rearguard action. Nevertheless, we were full of optimism. This was the early 1980s; we had the boats and the enthusiasm, idealism too – never an entirely good thing in business. Around this time we were approached by someone who had an idea that carrying grain by water from Tilbury Grain Terminal to Coxes Mill on the River Wey could be revived. We knew of Allied Mills, the biggest millers in the country and owners of a number of waterside mills, of which Coxes Mill was one. The company still had a certain amount of their imported grain delivered by inland barge to their various mills around the country, so they did not view suggestions regarding carriage by water with the suspicion that other companies often displayed.

Barges *Clinton* and *Anny* at Coxes Lock Mill unloading Canadian grain loaded in Tilbury.

Allied Mills now owned Coxes Mill. This was a mill which ground 'specialist' flours. It had received grain by barge from the turn of the nineteenth century until the late 1960s, but with the opening of Tilbury Grain Terminal further down the Thames it was deemed too far, too difficult, and too costly a job for the old wooden barges then employed to undertake. The Wey barges brought their last loads from London to the mill in 1969 and delivery was switched to rail, with Coxes having its own railhead brought straight into the mill grounds. Though Allied Mills received its grain in this way for more than ten years, by the 1980s the service had become unreliable; it was spasmodic, and British Rail often wanted to collect the emptied wagons at short notice. It was becoming expensive too. The company was already considering a switch to road transport, though this was a few years before the M25 was built, which meant a slow and difficult journey across London. When Allied Mills was approached about the possibility of reviving water transport the mill manager was willing to consider the idea, especially as the machinery originally installed in the 1930s for unloading the barges, powered by a huge single-cylinder Ruston engine, remained in situ.

They were interested. Could a trial run be undertaken? Of course, no problem, we said, though the actual logistics had yet to be worked out. To send narrow beamed canal boats to Tilbury was out of the question; it was too far and the boats too small to safely load overside, either from ships or the massive silos. On the other hand the 200-ton Dutch motor barge which was available to load the grain at the Terminal was far too big to reach Coxes Mill. Instead, it loaded at Tilbury, travelled up river as far as Sunbury-on-Thames and there, with the use of a hired auger, the grain was transhipped into a pair of our narrowboats, which could then complete the journey to the mill. Though the trials showed the idea to be feasible, in practice there were too many problems: there was nowhere to easily moor a loaded 200-ton barge for transhipment that far upstream; it took too long to move the grain from barge to narrowboat, and to do so was difficult and dangerous; the job involved too many people, took too much time and done in this way was just not economically viable.

Time for a rethink.

Two small motor barges were needed, each able to carry around 70 tons of cargo, robust enough to cope with the vicissitudes of loading so far down river, yet small enough to negotiate the two locks and several tight bridges of the River Wey up to the mill. Having secured the support of the National Trust, who by then managed the Wey Navigation, and the Thames Water Authority, which having superseded the old Thames Conservancy now controlled the Thames above Teddington, we had expected our major stumbling-block to be the entrenched organizations that exerted total control over what happened on the river below Teddington. The Port of London stretches some 95 miles, from just below Teddington Lock to its seaward limits in the Thames estuary. The whole length is governed by the Port of London Authority and was the stamping ground of the Honourable Company of Watermen and Lightermen, the Transport and General Workers Union and the London Dock Labour Board. It required the cooperation of all these different groups if we were to succeed in our bid to revive this defunct traffic.

We reasoned that all should welcome the return of such a long-standing traffic to the Thames, albeit in a changed form, using individual motor barges rather than dumb craft towed by a tug. Transport of any goods on the Thames had long been regarded as dock work, which could only be carried out by registered lightermen. Financially the job would not have been feasible if the lightermen insisted that they must have men on our barges. Thus, even after an interval of some ten years, resistance was expected from those who so vigorously opposed any new working practices and more modern forms of river transport. Stepping gingerly, knowing the militancy of the dock workers, we made our approach carefully. As it turned out, there was no need to persuade. It proved to be quite easy. The so-called 'eastabout-westabout charter' was cited: strangely this anachronistic and ancient piece of 'kingly' legislation, something which at that time we had never heard of, was to be our 'free pass'. In spite of determined opposition to any 'outsiders' seeking to use the river, and the PLA's fear of the strikes and walkouts by dockers and lightermen that were endemic at the time, all believed implicitly in the terms of the charter, which granted the freedom of the river to 'western' bargemen, and so were moved to give their reluctant support to our proposed venture.

So much for the power of history.

It proved rather more difficult to find craft of the right size: big enough to take sufficient cargo and load at Tilbury Grain Terminal, which was designed for much larger vessels, but also small enough to navigate the shallow and restricted waters of the Wey, to creep through its tight bridges and edge in and out of its small locks.

Eventually, in partnership with another carrier, two steel motor barges were found: one Dutch and one British, both built in the 1920s. Each had to be equipped for two crew living onboard. New wheelhouses were built to allow passage through the final bridge before the mill, engines were overhauled and navigation equipment installed. After considerable refurbishment of hulls and topsides, they were finally proudly painted in the company colours and ready to work.

Thus was waterborne freight revived, for a short period, in the 1980s. Cargoes of wheat loaded into the holds of barges were amongst the earliest freights ever to be transported on the river. Our own barges were not fundamentally different in shape, size or construction to the very first ones. The problems our crews encountered were similar to those of their forebears: passages were still determined by tide and current, flood or drought; the weirpool at the entrance to the Wey Navigation was just as intractable as it was in the past. Yet overall it was an economic and environmentally friendly form of transport which worked well. For over two years our barges delivered around 200 tons of imported Canadian Western Region hard wheat to the mill each week. amounting to over 10,000 tons per year. When the mill closed in 1983, it was for reasons unconnected with grain deliveries by water. Though among the very last to carry regular freight on inland waters and albeit by then trading on borrowed time, we were for a while a proud, though minuscule, part of a waterborne system that had kept London supplied with its daily bread for some 2,000 years.

Chapter Fifteen

A Proper Loaf of Bread

'Man has depended upon the wheat plant for himself and his
beasts for thousands of years. A global wheat failure would be a
disaster that few nations could survive for even one year.'
Symposium on Genetics and Breeding of Durum Wheat[1]

This statement made as recently as 2002, based on measured
research rather than alarmist premonition, does no more than
restate a constant fear that has existed since the beginning of time.

Thankfully most of us never need think too seriously about the
effect of famine upon ourselves personally. Indeed, here in Britain
we have almost forgotten that hunger can lead to starvation and
ultimately death; we've forgotten that food is what keeps us alive.
Eating has become an end in itself. Once, man's main concern was
how to fill his belly, not what he might choose for dinner that day.
For the timeless majority, an unvarying diet of grain in the form of
bread or porridge was all they would ever eat, and its continuing
availability was relied on for survival. Fear of hunger drove men,
and this condition, consciously or unconsciously, has impacted on
people's lives even until modern times.

During World War I Britain came close to starving. Hasty
research was undertaken, aimed at solving such problems as how
to keep bread fresh for troops in the trenches, how to conserve
supplies and minimize waste. Substitutes for wheat reminiscent
of the Middle Ages, such as mixtures of peas, arrowroot, parsnips,

beans, lentils, maize, rice, barley and oats, were used in bread making experiments. By 1917, sufficient numbers of grain ships were being sunk by submarines as they crossed the Atlantic that the nation was in dire peril of starvation. The government fixed a maximum price for bread and issued rules for reducing waste. Bakers were forbidden to sell bread until it was twelve hours old; no stale bread could be exchanged; only 'regulation' flour could be used, the millers preparing flour from such grains as the authorities provided, and under their control. Even the shape of loaves was decreed, and all fancy pastries were forbidden. Another order in 1918 directed that bakers should use a proportion of up to 20 percent of potatoes in their bread.

During World War II regulations were again imposed on the baking industry, and by its end most of Europe was seriously undernourished. Bread was rationed here in the UK within living memory, right up until the mid-twentieth century. Such episodes fade quickly from the collective consciousness, yet it is worth sparing a moment to consider how this driving force, the fear of hunger, conditioned the lives of our ancestors.

It was fear of starvation that drove rulers and regulators throughout the ages to try to find ways to protect the essential staple; to ensure that sufficient quantities of it reached the marketplace and that, once there, it was affordable by the great majority who depended upon it for their very survival.

The first laws passed in Britain concerned the supply of bread. A measuring system, essential once surplus was demanded, was based upon the single wheat grain. The natural right of navigation, preserved by Magna Carta and countless later statutes, ensured that moving grain by water took precedence over all other demands, no matter how powerful the claimant.

In England, the growing, harvesting and transporting of grain from where it was cultivated to where it would be consumed has not changed in essence for two thousand years. It is easy to see how particular events disrupted the pattern of everyday life and how people adjusted to the changes imposed upon them, yet whatever the circumstance the need for bread has remained constant.

A Proper Loaf of Bread

The twentieth century witnessed the demise of freight carried on inland waters in the UK, though much bulk grain is still carried on the rivers and canals of mainland Europe. Today the primal relationship between London, the capital city, and the Thames, our most favoured river, has almost faded to nothing. That symbiotic partnership once so crucial to the well-being and prosperity of both is broken. The Port of London finally succumbed to the inescapable demands of the modern world and London's wealth ceased to depend upon the huge quantity of goods brought to the city's doorstep by water. Its strategic position, once so vital on this river, has become largely irrelevant. Any grain still grown in its hinterlands goes elsewhere. The Thames is now a waterway devoted to leisure pursuits, and no longer the lifeblood which once sustained our most famous city. The working river, along with its busy world of boatmen and bargemen, dockers and lightermen, their vessels and their skills, is no more.

Only the need for wheat continues unabated. The people must still be fed and bread is still regarded as a daily essential. Now the grain market is global: grain supplies have tightened, become streamlined, demand has climbed, markets have been privatized and trade rules relaxed. Canadian grain continues to pour into the terminal at Tilbury, whilst large quantities of low protein grain, better suited to modern methods of bread making, is grown in Britain. Ships able to carry 60,000 tons of wheat are replacing the older 25,000 ton vessels. Ports edge ever closer to the sea; shipping channels have to be deepened, and grain terminals increase their loading and unloading capacities. The Port of Tilbury, 30 miles downstream of London, handles 1.4 million tons of grain annually and is still expanding.

Scarcely anything in our modern mills is reminiscent of their predecessors from the early days of the Industrial Revolution. They now produce hundreds of different types of flour for every conceivable application, and in incredible quantities. Every year, 320 million tons of wheat flour for human consumption alone run off the milling rollers. Wheat milling especially has become a global industry. The plant that was cultivated by the pioneers of agriculture over 10,000 years ago is now the staple food of a third of the world's population – a bulwark between us and hunger.

Today, this staple foodstuff has been transformed into an industrial triumph. Technology, thanks to the Chorleywood Bread Process, has found the cheapest way yet of feeding everyone their daily bread – though problematically, growing numbers of people are finding that this same daily bread makes them ill. We seem to have evolved an industrial bread making system that produces bread that more and more people cannot eat. Surely it is more than coincidence that the abrupt increase in coeliac disease, an allergic reaction to gluten first noted in the 1960s, made its appearance at much the same time that bread started to be made using the CBP?

Some would say that the pappy, bland nature of CBP bread is reason enough to consign it to the dustbin of food history, but the fact that it contains additives which go unlisted other than as 'processing aids' gives even further and possibly greater grounds for binning it. Over 80 percent of all British bread is now made using this method. Even bread not instantly identifiable as the reviled, plastic-wrapped white-sliced loaf, uses a process called 'activated dough development' (ADD), which involves a similar range of additives. Apart from a tiny percentage, this is the bread we eat today and have done so for over fifty years. Yet it is possible that this indigestible product has sown the seeds of its own destruction and is largely responsible for a rapidly growing and clearly lucrative industry which provides a range of gluten-free products, the most significant of which is that oxymoron, gluten-free bread.

Luckily for every action there is a reaction. It is no accident that out of a nutritional and culinary disaster has arisen an artisan bread movement that has spread across the globe. In the twentieth century one of the leading authorities on bread, French-born Raymond Calvel (incidentally the man who showed Julia Child how to make French bread with American ingredients) took a modern approach towards preserving and improving the ancient craft of bread making. He stood up for the rapidly diminishing traditions of bread making. A chemist by training, he advised that for the best yeast performance the amount of salt used in a bread recipe should be 1.8 percent of the weight of the flour.[2] He pointed out that for slow-fermenting breads, such as sourdoughs, what was important was not the quantity of gluten in a flour, but rather the quality, so that it could stand up to the long, slow rising times. His experiments revealed that mixing flour and water, then allowing this mixture to rest before adding yeast and salt, reduced the total mixing and kneading time required and resulted in 'bread that has a creamy crumb, excellent flavour, and very good quality overall'.

Fortunately for those who care about such things, the preserve of artisan bread makers today stretches way beyond the simple desire to make a good old-fashioned well-risen white loaf. Their interests encompass environmental and nutritional concerns. They have introduced new generations to a wider variety of grains, many organically grown. They have been innovative, bringing a whole new dimension to bread making, while at the same time returning to the original process of slow, natural fermentation, reminding us, once again, of the true wonder of bread.

My story is ended, along with that of those individuals once responsible for ensuring that a daily loaf of bread, no matter the vicissitudes of history with its shifts and reversals and instability, made it to everyone's table. Thankfully it ends on a positive note. We can still eat the bread of our forebears and I can still bake a celebration loaf, though sadly those grain barges that once so sparked the imagination no longer pass my window.

HOW TO MAKE A PROPER LOAF OF BREAD

This is the simplest possible yeasted dough. It can be worked into all kinds of shapes or augmented with other ingredients to produce different flavours and textures.

Ingredients:
600 g (1½ lbs) stoneground strong wholemeal flour
5 g (teaspoon) sea salt
320 ml (1½ cups) water

8 g fresh yeast
flour or seeds for the top

Makes 1 large or 2 small loaves

Weigh the flour and salt into a bowl. Measure the total amount of water and pour about a quarter of it into a small jug or bowl. Dissolve the yeast in this water by stirring it gently with your fingers. Pour the yeasty water into the bowl with the flour and salt and add the rest of the water. Use one hand to hold the bowl and the other to begin mixing the dough.

As soon as all the dry flour has become wet and the dough has begun to form, scrape it on to the worktop and begin kneading. Do not add any flour at this stage, even if the dough seems to you to be rather wet. If it seems too dry, add some more water. As you knead, the flour will absorb the water and the gluten structure should begin to develop. Knead for 10 to 15 minutes. Rather less time is needed if using a mixer. At the end of the mixing/kneading process, the dough should be soft, slightly silky to the touch and with a definite elasticity that was not there at the beginning.

Make sure the bowl is reasonably clean and put the dough back in it. The bowl should be big enough that when covered with a polythene bag or some clingfilm the rising dough doesn't come into contact with it. Leave the bowl in a warm place (around 25°C). After two hours, the dough should have risen appreciably. If it has grown significantly in less than two hours, you can either 'knock it back' by gently folding it over on itself a couple of times and leave it to rise again, or just progress to the next stage.

Grease one large loaf tin or two small ones with some fat or vegetable oil. Tip the dough onto the worktop again. If you plan to make two small loaves, divide the dough in half. Using the barest flick of flour to prevent the dough sticking to your hands or the worktop, roll it into a sausage about twice as long as the longest side of the tin. Flatten this sausage with your knuckles and then fold it in three. Again, knuckle the dough down until it is a flattish rectangle about two-thirds the length of your tin.

A Proper Loaf of Bread

Starting at the edge furthest from you, fold it over and roll it up, trying to keep the dough under some tension, but not folding it so tightly that it tears. Finish your roll with the seam underneath and then pick the whole thing up and place it in the tin. Set your bread to prove in a warm place, covered with a stiff plastic bag or large bowl to stop it drying out too much. It is important not to let the dough touch the cover as it rises otherwise it may stick and damage the loaf structure when the cover is removed.

Preheat the oven to 230°C or its hottest setting. When the dough has risen appreciably but still gives some resistance when gently pressed, put the loaf or loaves carefully into the oven. Bake for 30-40 minutes, turning the heat down to 200°C after 10 minutes.

Turn the bread out of the tin and check that it is done. Tap the bottom of the loaf and it should sound hollow. Also, check the 'shoulder' – where the side gives way to the domed top of the loaf – this is often the last area of crust to firm up. Gently push your finger into the shoulder – if it feels at all squashy, it needs a bit longer in the oven. If the bottom seems rather pale, turn the loaf out of its tin and put it on one of the oven's wire shelves to finish baking. When it is done, cool it on a rack to stop the bottom sweating and going soggy.[3]

Notes

CHAPTER 1

1. Anna Revedin et al, 'Thirty Thousand-Year-Old Evidence of Plant Food Processing.' Proceedings of the National Academy of Sciences of the United States of America 107.44 (2010): 18815–18819.
2. Ian Haynes, *Blood of the Provinces* (Oxford University Press, 2013), p. 176.
3. 'Medieval cuisine', Wikipedia (en.wikipedia.org/wiki/Medieval_cuisine).
4. 'A Brief History of Bread', Hungry History (www.history.com/news/hungry-history/a-brief-history-of-bread).
5. Edmond Bordeaux Szekely, *The Essene Gospel of Peace* (First Christians' (Essene) Church, 1970), p. 37.

CHAPTER 2

1. 'Medieval cuisine', op. cit.
2. Rachel Hartman, 'The Medieval Agricultural Year', *Strange Horizons*, No. 12, February (2001).
3. Ibid.
4. Ibid.
5. 'Quern-stone', Wikipedia (en.wikipedia.org/wiki/Quern-stone).
6. Camilla A. Dickson, and James Holms Dickson, *Plants and People in Ancient Scotland* (Stroud: Tempus Publishing, 2000), p.120.
7. Heather Smith, 'Celtic and Romano British Foods from the Isles: a General Approach' (www.academia.edu/1488019/Celtic_and_Romano_British_Foods_from_the_Isles-_a_General_Approach), p. 19.
8. Ibid., p. 20.
9. Ken Albala, 'Reconstructing Medieval Bread', Getty Iris Blog, 2015 (blogs.getty.edu/iris/reconstructing-medieval-bread).

CHAPTER 3

1. E.O. Gordon, *Prehistoric London, its Mounds and Circles* (Muskogee: Artisan Publishers, 1985), p. 113.
2. Gustav Milne, *The Port of Roman London* (London: Batsford, 1985).
3. 'London Bridge', Wikipedia (en.wikipedia.org/wiki/London_Bridge)
4. 'History of the Port of London pre 1908', Port of London Authority (www.pla.co.uk/Port-Trade/History-of-the-Port-of-London-pre-1908).
5. Ibid.
6. Peter Marsden, *Ships of the Port of London: First to Eleventh Centuries AD* (London: English Heritage, 1994), p. 81.
7. Victor Labate, 'Roman Mills', Ancient History Encyclopedia (www.ancient.eu/article/907/).
8. Robert Spain, 'A Possible Roman Tide Mill', Paper No. 5, Kent Archeological Society, 2002 (www.kentarchaeology.ac/authors/005.pdf).
9. Natasha Sheldon, 'Pompeian Bakeries', Ancient History and Archeology (www.ancienthistoryarchaeology.com/pompeian-bakeries).

10. Cristina Rosell, Joanna Bajerska and Aly F. el Sheikha (eds.), *Bread and its Fortification* (Boca Raton: Taylor & Francis, 2016), p. 4.
11. Ibid.

CHAPTER 4

1. Peter Marsden, op. cit., p. 81.
2. Gustav Milne, *The Port of Medieval London* (Stroud: Tempus Publishing, 2003), pp. 30-34.
3. J.R. Maddicott, 'London and Droitwich, c.650-750: trade, industry and the rise of Mercia', in *Anglo-Saxon England*, Vol. 34 (Cambridge University Press, 2005), pp. 8-9.
4 Ibid., p. 14.
5. Ibid., p. 44.
6. 'London and Westminster during the Norman period', History of London (www.thehistoryoflondon.co.uk/london-and-westminster-during-the-norman-period/).
7. Ibid.
8. Ibid.
9. 'Maslin bread' Oakden {oakden.co.uk/maslin-bread-recipe/).
10. Thomas Dawson, *A Good Huswifes Handmaide for the Kitchin* (London: Richard Jones, 1594).
11. 'Manchet bread recipe', Oakden (oakden.co.uk/manchet-bread-recipe/).

CHAPTER 5

1 'Everything starts with grain' (mu.ranter.net/design-theory/food-basis/everything-starts-with-grain).
2. Martha Carlin and Joel T. Rosenthal (eds.), *Food and Eating in Medieval Europe* (London: Hambledon Press, 1998), p. 120.
3. Jim Andrew, *Old Weights and Measures* (Birmingham Museum of Science & Industry, 2008), p. 3.
4. Nelson, Robert L. 'The Price of Bread: Poverty, Purchasing Power, and The Victorian Laborer's Standard of Living', Victorian Web (www.victorianweb.org/history/work/nelson1.html).
5. 'Black Death in England', Wikipedia (en.wikipedia.org/wiki/Black_Death_in_England).
6. David Routt, 'The Economic Impact of the Black Death', Economic History Association (eh.net/encyclopedia/the-economic-impact-of-the-black-death).
7. Ibid.
8. From a recipe by Carolyn Priest-Dorman (www.cs.vassar.edu/~capriest/vikbagels.html).

CHAPTER 6

1. James Frederick Edwards, *The Transport System of Medieval England and Wales: A Geographical Synthesis*, Doctoral Thesis, University of Salford, Department of Geography, 1987. pp. 265-6.
2. 'History of Watermills', Jesmond Dene Old Mill (www.jesmonddeneoldmill.org.uk/mill/technology.html).

Notes

3. Ibid.
4. Fred S. Thacker, *The Thames Highway: A History of Inland Navigation* (London: Thacker, 1914), p. 46.
5. This and subsequent quotes, ibid., pp. 52-53.
6. 'Halers and Horses: Working Western Barges' (www.victoriacountyhistory. ac.uk/explore/sites/explore/files/explore_assets/2010/03/22/Working_western_ Barges.pdf).
7. Charles Knight (ed.), *London*, Vol. III (London: Knight, 1842), p. 365.
8. Ibid., pp. 365-66.
9. Ibid., p. 366.

CHAPTER 7

1. John Langdon, 'The Efficiency of Inland Water Transport in Medieval England', in *Waterways and Canal-Building in Medieval England*, (ed.) John Blair (Oxford University Press, 2007), p. 128.
2. Simon, Townley, *Henley-on-Thames: Town, Trade and River* (Chichester: Phillimore, 2009), pp. 78-104.
3. Ibid.
4. 'Halers and Horses: Working Western Barges', op. cit.
5. Ibid.
6. 'London Bridge', Dragonwing (midtown.net/dragonwing/col9802.htm).
7. Buchanan Sharp, *Famine and Scarcity in Late Medieval and Early Modern England: The Regulation of Grain Marketing, 1256-1631* (Cambridge University Press, 2016), p. 103.
8. Ibid., p. 106.

CHAPTER 8

1. Bruce Robinson, 'London: Brighter Lights, Bigger City' (www.bbc.co.uk/ history/british/civil_war_revolution/brighter_lights_01.shtml).
2. *A General Estimate of the Corn Trade, Addressed to the Lord Mayor* (London: Cooper, 1758), p.28.
3. David Carmichael, 'Grain Provision in the City of London in the early Seventeenth Century', Paper presented at the LSE, Institute of Historical Research, School of Advanced Study, 2013, pp. 2-3 (www.lse.ac.uk/ economicHistory/seminars/EH590Workshop/EH590ST2013/Camichael.pdf).
4. Ibid., p. 26.
5. 'Great Plague of London', Wikipedia (en.wikipedia.org/wiki/Great_Plague_ of_London).
6. Daniel Defoe, *A Journal of the Plague Year* (London: E. Nutt, 1722), p. 93.
7. Ibid., pp. 125-28.
8. 'Records of the Company of Watermen and Lightermen', City of London (www.cityoflondon.gov.uk/things-to-do/london-metropolitan-archives/ visitor-information/Documents/18-records-of-the-company-of-watermen-and- lightermen.pdf).
9. Gavin Weightman, *London's Thames: The River That Shaped a City and Its History* (St. Martin's Press, 2006).
10. 'Great Fire of London' (royalalstrup1128.myfeedportal.com/i/great_fire_of_

Notes

london).

11. 'Great Plague of London', Wikipedia.
12. Thomas Austin (ed.), *Two Fifteenth-Century Cookery-Books* (Oxford University Press, 1964), p. 52.
13. Cindy Renfrow, *Take a Thousand Eggs or More* (Unionville: Royal Fireworks Press, 2003).
14. Maxime de la Falaise, *Seven Centuries of English Cooking* (New York: Grove Press, 1994).

CHAPTER 9

1. Daniel Defoe, *A Tour Thro' the Whole Island of Great Britain* (London: Strahan, 1724), p. 71.
2. Ibid., p. 67.
3. Dennis Baker, 'The Marketing of Corn in the First Half of the Eighteenth Century: North-East Kent', *The Agricultural History Review*, Vol. 18, No. 2 (1970), p. 129.
4. John Boys, *General View of the Agriculture of the County of Kent* (London: B. McMillan, 1805), p. 203.
5. Daniel Defoe, *A Tour Thro' the Whole Island of Great Britain*, op. cit., p. 142.
6. Dennis Baker, op. cit., p. 130.
7. Ibid., pp. 133-34.
8. Ibid., p. 136.
9. Quoted in Mark Overton, *Agricultural Revolution in England* (Cambridge University Press, 1996), p. 144.
10. Dennis Baker, op. cit., p. 142.
11. Ibid., p.143.
12. From a recipe by Jennifer Stanley (savoringthepast.net/2016/07/23/the-best-bread-pudding-yet/).
13. Elizabeth Raffald, *The Experienced English Housekeeper* (London: R. Baldwin 1786), p. 316.
14. Ibid., p. 292.

CHAPTER 10

1. Peter Ackroyd. *Thames: Sacred River* (London: Vintage, 2008).
2. 'Locks and Weirs on the River Thames', Wikipedia (en.wikipedia.org/wiki/Locks_and_weirs_on_the_River_Thames)
3. Thomas Allen, *The History and Antiquities of London, Westminster, Southwark* (London, George Virtue, 1839), p. 475.
4. Paul Sharp, 'The Long American Grain Invasion of Britain: Market Integration and the Wheat Trade Between North America and Britain from the Eighteenth Century', Discussion Paper, No. 08-20, Dept. of Economics, University of Copenhagen (www.economics.ku.dk/research/publications/wp/2008/0820.pdf).
5. Glenn A. Knoblock, *The American Clipper Ship, 1845-1920: A Comprehensive History, with a Listing of Builders and their Ships* (North Carolina: McFarland, 2014).
6. 'Pool of London', Wikipedia (en.wikipedia.org/wiki/Pool_of_London).

Notes

CHAPTER 11

1. 'Illustration of Fire in London', British Library (www.bl.uk/collection-items/illustration-of-fire-in-london-albion-mills).
2. 'History of the Port of London pre 1908', op. cit.
3. 'Lighterman', Wikipedia (en.wikipedia.org/wiki/Lighterman).
4. 'History of the Port of London pre 1908', op. cit.
5. Bill Bryson, *At Home: A Short History of Private Life* (Doubleday, 2011), p. 125.
6. Isabella Beeton, *Mrs Beeton's Book of Household Management* (Oxford World Classics, 2000), p. 336.
7. Paul Hollywood, 'English Muffins', BBC (www.bbc.co.uk/food/recipes/english_muffins_56640).

CHAPTER 12

1. 'Thames steamers', Wikipedia (en.wikipedia.org/wiki/Thames_steamers).
2. 'History of the Port of London pre 1908', op. cit.
3. 'Thames Embankment', Wikipedia (en.wikipedia.org/wiki/Thames_Embankment).
4. 'History of the Port of London pre 1908', op. cit.
5. Ibid.
6. *Port of London Act*, 1908, Ch. 68, p. 3.
7. 'History of the Port of London pre 1908', op. cit.
8. Frank Mulville, 'The Highly Refined Thames Barge Knew Her Worth', *Cruising World*, January (1983), p. 89.
9. Ibid., p. 90.
10. Ibid.
11. 'Tollesbury', Association of Dunkirk Little Ships (www.adls.org.uk/t1/node/521).
12. Frank Mulville, op. cit., pp. 90-91.
13. 'Canal and river barges of South East England', Canal Junction (www.canaljunction.com/craft/thames_barge.htm).
14. David Gordon Wilson, *The Thames: Record of a Working Waterway* (London: B.T. Batsford, 1987), p. 108.
15. Maria Eliza Rundell, *A New System of Domestic Cookery* (London: John Murray, 1809), p. 245.
16. Dr A. Hunter, *Receipts in Modern Cookery* (York: Wilson and Spence, 1806), p. 117.
17. 'British Wartime Foor' Cook's Info (www.cooksinfo.com/british-wartime-food).
18. 'National Loaf', Wikipedia (en.wikipedia.org/wiki/National_Loaf).

CHAPTER 13

1. David Rose, 'Life on the Wey Navigations', The Guildford Dragon News (www.guildford-dragon.com/2012/02/27/life-on-the-wey-navigations)
2. Daniel Defoe, *A Tour Thro' the Whole Island of Great Britain*, op. cit., p. 87.
3. David Rose, 'Life on the Wey Navigations', op. cit.
4. Ibid.
5. 'Wey and Goldalming Navigations', Wikipedia (en.wikipedia.org/wiki/Wey_

and_Godalming_Navigations)
6. This and subsequent quotations, Nancy Larcombe (ed.), *Captain White's River Life* (Towed Haul, 1985).
7. 'Wey and Goldalming Navigations', op. cit.
8. 'Coxes Lock', Wikipedia (en.wikipedia.org/wiki/Coxes_Lock)
9. 'Baker's Apprentice', George Weston Ltd (www.weston.ca/PDF/GWL_History_Bakers_Apprentice.pdf).
10. Ibid.
11. 'Britain's Biggest Baker', George Weston Ltd (www.weston.ca/PDF/GWL_History_Britains_Biggest_Baker.pdf).
12. Ibid.
13. Ibid.
14. 'Wey Navigation New Haw to Coxes Lock' (www.weyriver.co.uk/theriver/wey_nav_8.htm).
15. Andrew Whitley, *Bread Matters* (London: Fourth Estate, 2006).

CHAPTER 15

1. Ardeshir B. Damania, 'Durum wheat cultivation and use in the USA with special reference to California', in *Proceedings of the International Symposium on Genetics and Breeding of Durum Wheat* (Bari: CIHEAM, 2014).
2. Raymond Calvel, *The Taste of Bread: A Translation of Le Goût du pain* (New York: Springer, 2001), p. 19.
3. Andrew Whitley, op. cit.

List of illustrations

Bibliography

A General Estimate of the Corn Trade, Addressed to the Lord Mayor (London: Cooper, 1758).

Ackroyd, Peter. *London: The Biography* (London: Chatto & Windus, 2000).

Ackroyd, Peter. *Thames: Sacred River* (London: Vintage, 2008).

Albala, Ken. 'Reconstructing Medieval Bread', Getty Iris Blog, 2015 (blogs.getty.edu/iris/reconstructing-medieval-bread).

Aldrete, Gregory S. *Daily Life in the Roman City: Rome, Pompeii, and Ostia* (Connecticut: Greenwood Press, 2004).

Allen, Thomas. *The History and Antiquities of London, Westminster, Southwark* (London, George Virtue, 1839).

Andrew, Jim. *Old Weights and Measures* (Birmingham Museum of Science & Industry, 2008).

Ashton, John. *The History of Bread*, (London: Religious Tract Society, 1904).

Atkin, Michael. *The International Grain Trade* (Cambridge: Woodhead Publishing, 1992).

Austin, Thomas (ed.). *Two Fifteenth-Century Cookery-Books* (Oxford University Press, 1964).

Bailey, Adrian. *The Blessings of Bread* (London: Paddington Press, 1975).

Baker, Dennis. 'The Marketing of Corn in the First Half of the Eighteenth Century: North-East Kent', *The Agricultural History Review*, Vol. 18, No. 2 (1970), pp. 126-150.

Beeton, Isabella. *Mrs Beeton's Book of Household Management* (Oxford World Classics, 2000).

Boys, John. *General View of the Agriculture of the County of Kent* (London: B. McMillan, 1805).

Bryson, Bill. *At Home: A Short History of Private Life* (Doubleday, 2011).

Burton, Frances D. *Fire: The Spark that Ignited Human Evolution* (Albuquerque: University of New Mexico Press, 2009).

Burton, John. *The Present State of Navigation on the Thames Considered; and Certain Regulations Proposed by a Commissioner* (Oxford: Daniel Prince, 1764).

Calvel, Raymond. *The Taste of Bread: A Translation of Le Goût du pain* (New York: Springer, 2001).

Campbell, Bruce M.S. *English Seigniorial Agriculture 1250-1450* (Cambridge University Press, 2000).

Campbell, Bruce M.S., James A. Galloway, Derek Keene, and Margaret Murphy. *A Medieval Capital and its Grain Supply: Agrarian Production and Distribution in the London Region c.1300* (London: Historical Geography Research Series, Research Paper Series, No.30, 1993).

Bibliography

Carlin, Martha and Joel T. Rosenthal (eds.). *Food and Eating in Medieval Europe* (London: Hambledon Press, 1998).

Carmichael, David. 'Grain Provision in the City of London in the early Seventeenth Century', Paper presented at the LSE, Institute of Historical Research, School of Advanced Study, 2013 (www.lse.ac.uk/economicHistory/seminars/EH590Workshop/EH590ST2013/Camichael.pdf).

Chapman, John. 'The River Thames: Regulatory Authorities' (http://www.project-purley.eu/R200234.pdf).

Cookson, Mildred M. and Claire Wooldridge. *From Quern to Computer: A History of Flour Milling* (Reading: The Mills Archive Archive Trust, 2016).

Cruyningen, Piet van and Erik Thoen (eds.). *Food Supply, Demand and Trade: Aspects of the Economic Relationship between Town and Countryside, Middle Ages to Nineteenth Century* (Turnhout: Brepols, 2012).

De la Falaise, Maxime. *Seven Centuries of English Cooking* (New York: Grove Press, 1994).

Defoe, Daniel. *A Journal of the Plague Year* (London: E. Nutt, 1722).

Defoe, Daniel. *A Tour Thro' the Whole Island of Great Britain* (London: Strahan, 1724).

Dickson, Camilla A., and James Holms Dickson. *Plants and People in Ancient Scotland* (Stroud: Tempus Publishing, 2000).

Edwards, James Frederick. *The Transport System of Medieval England and Wales: A Geographical Synthesis*, Doctoral Thesis, University of Salford, Department of Geography, 1987.

Evans, L.T. and W.J. Peacock (eds.). *Wheat Science: Today and Tomorrow* (Cambridge University Press, 1981).

Ferriotto, Mariana. 'The Regeneration of London's Dockland: New Riverside Regeneration or Catylist for Social Conflict?', Università degli Studi di Padova, 2015 (tesi.cab.unipd.it/47923/1/Tesi_Magistrale_Feriotto_Marianna_1046538_pdf.pdf).

Frantzen, Allen J. *Food, Eating and Identity in Early Medieval England* (Rochester: Boydell Press, 2014).

Galloway James A. and Margaret Murphy. 'Feeding the City: Medieval London and its Agrarian Hinterland,' *The London Journal*, Vol. 16, No. 1 (1991).

Gordon, E.O. *Prehistoric London, its Mounds and Circles* (Muskogee: Artisan Publishers, 1985).

Gras, Norman S.B. *The Evolution of the English Corn Market: From the Twelfth to the Eighteenth Century* (Cambridge: Harvard University Press, 1915).

Hartman, Rachel. 'The Medieval Agricultural Year', *Strange Horizons*, No. 12, February (2001).

Haynes, Ian. *Blood of the Provinces* (Oxford University Press, 2013).

Higham, Nicholas J. and Martin J. Ryan (eds.). *Place-Names, Language and the Anglo-Saxon Landscape* (Woodbridge: The Boydell Press, 2011).

Hobhouse, Hermione (ed.). *Survey of London: Poplar, Blackwall and Isle of Dogs*, Vols. 43 and 44 (London County Council, 1994) (www.british-history.ac.uk/survey-london/vols43-4).

Bibliography

Horrox, Rosemary (ed.). *The Black Death* (Manchester University Press, 1994).

Household, Humphrey. *The Thames and Severn Canal* (Stroud: Amberley Publishing, 2009).

Hunter, Dr A. *Receipts in Modern Cookery* (York: Wilson and Spence, 1806).

Jones, David H. 'How Tide Mills Work', in *Open to Tide Mills, Proceedings of an International Conference* (London: River Lea Tidal Mill Trust, 2000).

Knight, Charles (ed.), *London*, Vol. III (London: Knight, 1842).

Knoblock, Glenn A. *The American Clipper Ship, 1845-1920: A Comprehensive History, with a Listing of Builders and their Ships* (North Carolina: McFarland, 2014).

Labate, Victor. 'Roman Mills', Ancient History Encyclopedia (www.ancient.eu/article/907/).

Langdon, John. 'The Efficiency of Inland Water Transport in Medieval England', in *Waterways and Canal-Building in Medieval England*, (ed.) John Blair (Oxford University Press, 2007).

Larcombe, Nancy (ed.). *Captain White's River Life* (Towed Haul, 1985).

Leasor, James. *The Plague and the Fire* (London: George Allen and Unwin, 1962).

Loyn, H.R. *Anglo Saxon England and the Norman Conquest* (London: Routledge, 1962).

Maddicott, J.R. 'London and Droitwich, c.650-750: trade, industry and the rise of Mercia', in *Anglo-Saxon England*, Vol. 34 (Cambridge University Press, 2005).

Maddicott, J.R. 'Plague in Seventh-Century England', *Past and Present*, Vol. 156 (1997), pp. 7-54.

Marsden, Peter. *Ships of the Port of London: First to Eleventh Centuries AD* (London: English Heritage, 1994).

Mavor, William. *The General View of Agriculture in Berkshire* (London: Richard Phillips, 1809).

Millet, Martin. *The Romanization of Britain* (Cambridge University Press, 1990).

Milne, Gustav. *The Port of Roman London* (London: Batsford, 1985).

Milne, Gustav. *The Port of Medieval London* (Stroud: Tempus Publishing, 2003).

Muldrew, Craig. *Food, Energy and the Creation of Industriousness: Work and Material Culture in Agrarian England, 1550-1780* (Cambridge University Press, 2011).

Mulville, Frank. 'The Highly Refined Thames Barge Knew Her Worth', *Cruising World*, January (1983), pp. 88-91.

Nelson, Robert L. 'The Price of Bread: Poverty, Purchasing Power, and The Victorian Laborer's Standard of Living', Victorian Web (www.victorianweb.org/history/work/nelson1.html).

Overton, Mark. *Agricultural Revolution in England* (Cambridge University Press, 1996).

Pollan, Michael. *Cooked: A Natural History of Transformation* (London: Penguin Books, 2014).

Bibliography

Raffald, Elizabeth. *The Experienced English Housekeeper* (London: R. Baldwin 1786).

Renfrow, Cindy. *Take a Thousand Eggs or More* (Unionville: Royal Fireworks Press, 2003).

Revedin, Anna et al. 'Thirty Thousand-Year-Old Evidence of Plant Food Processing', Proceedings of the National Academy of Sciences of the United States of America 107.44 (2010): 18815–18819.

Robinson, Bruce. 'London: Brighter Lights, Bigger City' (www.bbc.co.uk/history/british/civil_war_revolution/brighter_lights_01.shtml).

Robinson, Bruce. 'London's Burning' (www.bbc.co.uk/history/british/civil_war_revolution/great_fire_01.shtml).

Rose, David. *Guildford Our Town* (Derby: Breedon Books, 2001).

Rose, David. 'Life on the Wey Navigations', The Guildford Dragon News (www.guildford-dragon.com/2012/02/27/life-on-the-wey-navigations).

Rosell, Cristina, Joanna Bajerska and Aly F. el Sheikha (eds.), *Bread and its Fortification* (Boca Raton: Taylor & Francis, 2016).

Rothstein, Morton. *Centralizing Firms and Spreading Markets: The World of International Grain Traders 1846-1914* (University of California, 1988).

Routt, David. 'The Economic Impact of the Black Death', Economic History Association (eh.net/encyclopedia/the-economic-impact-of-the-black-death).

Rule, Fiona. *London's Docklands: A History of the Lost Quarter* (Hersham: Ian Allan Publishing, 2009).

Rule, Margaret and Jason Monaghan. *A Gallo-Roman Trading Vessel from Guernsey: The Excavation and Recovery of a Third Century Shipwreck* (Guernsey Museums and Galleries, 1993).

Rundell, Maria Eliza. *A New System of Domestic Cookery* (London: John Murray, 1809).

Sharp, Buchanan. *Famine and Scarcity in Late Medieval and Early Modern England: The Regulation of Grain Marketing, 1256-1631* (Cambridge University Press, 2016).

Sharp, Paul. 'The Long American Grain Invasion of Britain: Market Integration and the Wheat Trade Between North America and Britain from the Eighteenth Century', Discussion Paper, No. 08-20, University of Copenhagen (www.economics.ku.dk/research/publications/wp/2008/0820.pdf).

Sheldon, Natasha. 'Pompeian Bakeries', Ancient History and Archeology (www.ancienthistoryarchaeology.com/pompeian-bakeries).

Shepherd, Deborah J. *Daily Life in Arthurian Britain* (Westport: Greenwood Press, 2013).

Shrewsbury, J.F.D. *A History of Bubonic Plague* (Cambridge University Press, 1971).

Singman, Jeffrey L. *Daily Life in Medieval Europe* (Westport: Greenwood Press, 1999).

Singman, Jeffrey L. and Will McLean. *Daily Life in Chaucer's England* (Westport: Greenwood Press, 1995).

Smith, Heather. 'Celtic and Romano British Foods from the Isles: a General

Bibliography

Approach' (www.academia.edu/1488019/Celtic_and_Romano_British_Foods_
from_the_Isles-_a_General_Approach).

Spain, Robert. 'A Possible Roman Tide Mill', Paper No. 5, Kent Archeological
Society, 2002 (www.kentarchaeology.ac/authors/005.pdf).

Szekely, Edmond Bordeaux. *The Essene Gospel of Peace* (First Christians' (Essene)
Church, 1970).

Thacker, Fred S. *The Thames Highway: A History of Inland Navigation* (London:
Thacker, 1914).

Thornbury, Walter. *Old and New London* (London: Cassell, Petter & Galpin,
1878).

Townley, Simon. *Henley-on-Thames: Town, Trade and River* (Chichester: Phillimore,
2009).

Westerfield, R. B. 'Middlemen in English Business, Particularly Between 1660 and
1760', *Transactions Connecticut Academy of Arts and Sciences*, XIX, Connecticut
(1915).

Wheals, Brian Brenchley. *Theirs Were But Human Hearts* (Buckinghamshire: H.S.
Publishing, 1984).

Whitley, Andrew. *Bread Matters* (London: Fourth Estate, 2006).

Wilson, David Gordon. *The Thames: Record of a Working Waterway* (London: B.T.
Batsford, 1987).

Wood, Jacqui. *Prehistoric Cooking* (Stroud: Tempus, 2001).

Wrangham, Richard. *Catching Fire: How Cooking Made Us Human* (London:
Profile Books, 2009).

General Online Resources

"A Brief History of Bread', Hungry History (www.history.com/news/hungry-
history/a-brief-history-of-bread)

'Baker's Apprentice', George Weston Ltd (www.weston.ca/PDF/GWL_History_
Bakers_Apprentice.pdf)

'Black Death in England', Wikipedia (en.wikipedia.org/wiki/Black_Death_in_
England)

'Bread', Wikipedia (en.wikipedia.org/wiki/Bread)

'Britain's Biggest Baker', George Weston Ltd (www.weston.ca/PDF/GWL_
History_Britains_Biggest_Baker.pdf)

'British Wartime Food' Cook's Info (www.cooksinfo.com/british-wartime-food)

'Canal and river barges of South East England', Canal Junction (www.
canaljunction.com/craft/thames_barge.htm)

'Coxes Lock', Wikipedia (en.wikipedia.org/wiki/Coxes_Lock)

'English Muffins', BBC (www.bbc.co.uk/food/recipes/english_muffins_56640)

'Everything starts with grain' (mu.ranter.net/design-theory/food-basis/everything-
starts-with-grain)

Bibliography

'Great Fire of London' (royalalstrup1128.myfeedportal.com/i/great_fire_of_london)

'Great Plague of London', Wikipedia (en.wikipedia.org/wiki/Great_Plague_of_London)

'Halers and Horses: Working Western Barges' (www.victoriacountyhistory.ac.uk/explore/sites/explore/files/explore_assets/2010/03/22/Working_western_Barges.pdf)

'Henley and the Thames River Trade', Victoria County History (www.victoriacountyhistory.ac.uk/explore/items/henley-and-thames-river-trade)

'History of the Port of London pre 1908', Port of London Authority (www.pla.co.uk/Port-Trade/History-of-the-Port-of-London-pre-1908)

'The History of Watermills', Jesmond Dene Old Mill (www.jesmonddeneoldmill.org.uk/mill/technology.html)

'Illustration of Fire in London', British Library (www.bl.uk/collection-items/illustration-of-fire-in-london-albion-mills)

'Lighterman', Wikipedia (en.wikipedia.org/wiki/Lighterman)

'Locks and Weirs on the River Thames', Wikipedia (en.wikipedia.org/wiki/Locks_and_weirs_on_the_River_Thames)

'London Bridge', Dragonwing (midtown.net/dragonwing/col9802.htm)

'London Bridge', Wikipedia (en.wikipedia.org/wiki/London_Bridge)

'London and Westminster during the Norman period', History of London (www.thehistoryoflondon.co.uk/london-and-westminster-during-the-norman-period/)

'Medieval cuisine', Wikipedia (en.wikipedia.org/wiki/Medieval_cuisine).

'National Loaf', Wikipedia (en.wikipedia.org/wiki/National_Loaf)

'Pool of London', Wikipedia (en.wikipedia.org/wiki/Pool_of_London)

'Quern-stone', Wikipedia (en.wikipedia.org/wiki/Quern-stone)

'Records of the Company of Watermen and Lightermen', City of London (www.cityoflondon.gov.uk/things-to-do/london-metropolitan-archives/visitor-information/Documents/18-records-of-the-company-of-watermen-and-lightermen.pdf)

'Roman Britain: a Consideration of the Process of Romanization', British Museum (www.britishmuseum.org/PDF/british_museum_roman_britain.pdf)

'Thames Embankment', Wikipedia (en.wikipedia.org/wiki/Thames_Embankment)

'Thames steamers', Wikipedia (en.wikipedia.org/wiki/Thames_steamers)

'Tollesbury', Association of Dunkirk Little Ships (www.adls.org.uk/t1/node/521)

'Weston Family', Wikipedia (en.wikipedia.org/wiki/Weston_family)

'Wey and Goldalming Navigations', Wikipedia (en.wikipedia.org/wiki/Wey_and_Godalming_Navigations)

'Wey Navigation New Haw to Coxes Lock' (www.weyriver.co.uk/theriver/wey_nav_8.htm)

Alphabetical Index of Recipes

Index

Index

Index

102, 106, 215

middlemen, 94, 108, 125, 128, 131

Model Bakery, 196

Napoleonic Wars, 142

National loaf, 179

National Trust, 193, 213

Normans, 50, 54-5, 63, 67, 81

Ordinance of Labourers, 70

Orwell (river), 171

Oxford, 40, 52, 53, 77, 79, 82, 85, 87, 94, 96, 98, 113, 121, 135, 136, 139, 175

Oxford Canal, 136, 175

parched grain, 19, 20

Peasants' Revolt, 70

Pepys, Samuel, 116

plague, 12, 52, 55, 69, 71, 72, 108-10, 114, 116, 122

Pool of London, 38, 39, 97, 115, 145-6, 150, 167, 172, 173

Port of London, 90, 109, 115, 140, 146, 151-2, 154, 168-71, 176, 210, 213, 217

Port of London Act, 170

Port of London Authority, 115, 151, 170, 193, 213

Putney, 185

quartern loaf, 67

quern-stones, 30, 31, 34, 44

Queenhithe, 41, 97, 101, 107, 127

railways, 144-5, 154, 161, 165, 174-5, 187, 206

Reading, 77, 80, 122, 135, 174-5

river tolls, 51, 53, 86, 99, 136, 137, 182, 187

Royal Commission, 170

roller milling, 160, 161-2, 199, 217

Romans, 15, 27, 32, 34, 37, 39-45, 47-52, 55, 63, 78

Romano-Celtic ships, 42

Rooseveldt, Eleanor, 179

Rose & Co, 209, 210

salt trade, 52-3, 68, 122

shipbuilding, 42, 51, 166

Simmond's brewery, 175

Soke rights, 81

Sonning Mill, 175, 176

Soyer, Alexis, 163

Staines, 77, 78, 136, 139, 169, 175

Statute of Labourers, 70

Stort (river), 171, 205

Stour (river), 80, 124, 171

Suez Canal, 166

Tacitus, 41

Teddington, 77-8, 137, 170-1, 175, 176, 189, 190, 213

Tewkesbury, 136

Thames (river), 7, 12, 37-46, 52-53, 55, 67, 72, 76, 77-91, 106, 107, 114, 116, 121, 124, 136-7, 139, 149, 154, 158, 165, 168-177, 181-2, 185-7, 190, 193, 201-4, 206-8, 212-3, 217

Thames barges, 43, 172, 203

Thames Navigation Commission, 90, 136,174

Thames Conservancy, 115, 137, 169, 170, 174, 175, 213

Thames Lock, 184, 186, 190

Thames and Severn Canal, 135, 136, 174, 175

three field system, 64

tide mills, 12, 43, 123

Tilbury, 52, 77, 151, 154, 193, 207, 211, 212, 217

Tilbury Grain Terminal, 11, 181, 210, 212, 214, 217

towpath, 88, 99, 136, 190, 206

Transport and General Workers Union, 213

tugs, 166, 168-9, 175, 185, 187, 191, 201-2, 206

Vikings, 20, 51, 54, 72

watermen, 111, 112, 114-5, 154, 165,